Instrumental Music for Dyslexics
A Teaching Handbook

Instrumental Music for Dyslexics
A Teaching Handbook

Sheila M. Oglethorpe LRAM, GRSM, Dip RSA

Consultant in Dyslexia: Professor Margaret Snowling
University of York

Whurr Publishers

© 1996 Whurr Publishers Ltd
First published 1996 by
Whurr Publishers Ltd
19b Compton Terrace, London N1 2UN, England

British Library Cataloguing in Publication Data
A catalogue record for this book is available from the
British Library

ISBN 1-897635-69-9

Printed and bound in the UK by Athenaeum Press Ltd,
Gateshead, Tyne & Wear

Contents

Foreword

Instrumental Music for Dyslexics will be invaluable to everyone who is seeking clear and concise information about dyslexia and its problems, with particular emphasis on the hazards faced by dyslexic music pupils.

This book is the result of wide experience and research into ways to make music accessible to dyslexic pupils. Its imaginative and caring approach will help the teacher find new ways of getting around both confusion and lapses of memory, with its suggestions, ingenious ideas, exercises and strategies for meeting and overcoming these problems. Pupils gain immeasurably when encouraged to make discoveries and when possible, to use their own words to name them. Learning becomes an exciting experience when real communication between teacher and pupil is created.

The focus of this book is on teaching a keyboard instrument, however the text is extremely adaptable and usable for different musical instruments and for singing at all grades. It almost goes without saying that both teachers and pupils will need endless patience to achieve results. It is through willing and mutual effort that understanding and creativity arise resulting in a sense of relief for pupils once they realise that their difficulties are understood and allowances made for them. It is because all the stages are worked through together that doors can become unlocked and music made and shared in a special way,

Sheila Oglethorpe is to be congratulated upon her enlightened and inspiring way of writing, and for producing such an encouraging and heartening book.

Margaret Hubicki
MBE FRAM FRSA

Acknowledgements

This book would not have been written without the tireless help and patience of my husband Bill. I am immensely grateful to him, to my whole family for their interest and encouragement and in particular to our son Justin for his editorial help.

Many others have given invaluable assistance. I am especially grateful to Suzannah Stratton who has patiently supplied many details, to Rosamund Bromley who produced the fingering diagrams for the voilinists, to John Upton who did the music illustrations, to Robert Owen who gave me his ideas for scale notation and to Susan Druce who gave me the confidence to start.

I also owe a special debt of gratitude to Derek Aviss, David Halls, Christopher Helyer, Jill Holmes, Pat Legg, Kate Lloyd-Jones, Pamela Moore, Diana Tickell and to my two wonderful advisers Margaret Hubicki and Margaret Snowling who have given me unstinting encouragement and assistance.

There are many others whom I have not mentioned by name, in particular my pupils to whom I owe so much and who have taught me and inspired me daily.

I thank you all.

Sheila M. Oglethorpe
April 1996

Preface

Throughout this work, I have used the term '*dyslexia*' as being synonymous with Sp L D (*specific learning difficulties*). This is a controversial area; the argument for and against the use of either term is not one in which I am qualified to partake. Dyslexia may be considered by some researchers to have a narrower interpretation than does Sp L D, but it allows the adjective 'dyslexic', which is why I have chosen to use it.

The main focus of this book is on pupils who fall between the ages of about 6 or 7 and 13. These are the crucial years, when the acquisition of literacy is very much to the fore and dyslexic children are learning to come to terms with their dyslexia. It is also a time when the pressures of academic examinations seem far away and many children are keen to try out almost anything that is suggested to them, hence the huge numbers of budding young musicians, many of whom eventually aspire to playing in youth orchestras and go on, possibly, into the world of the professional.

By the time a pupil has reached this exalted stage, he will, if he is dyslexic, have learnt a series of strategies that will help him to cope in the world belonging to those who are not dyslexic. There will be some who will argue that he has 'grown out of' his dyslexia, but that is not necessarily, if ever, the case. It is more likely that he will have reached a compromise with his dyslexia and he will have evolved ways of learning or behaving that will enable him to be equal to the challenges he faces.

The teenage pupil is usually more articulate with regard to his own feelings than is the younger child. He is better able to communicate to the teacher what his difficulties are and what he feels about them. He may have reached the stage when both he and his teacher feel comfortable with one another and can work things out together, knowing what the difficulties are likely to be and having discovered ways of either overcoming or avoiding them. This is the stage that requires no help from a book, although the strategies that may be employed to surmount the difficulties will be the same as those for younger pupils.

It is for the teacher of the dyslexic pupil, who is going through the difficult years of recognition of his limitations and yet who aspires to the hopes and expectations of his non-dyslexic peers, that this book is written.

It is not easy for the instrumental teacher to break out of her world. Teaching music, other than class music, runs parallel with other 'academic' teaching, but the relationship is not an easy one and the instrumental music teacher often feels herself to be rather isolated. In many schools, instrumental lessons can interfere with 'academic' subjects, which naturally upsets the teachers of those subjects, or the music teacher is obliged to teach in break periods, dinner hours or after school, thereby ensuring that she does not meet her colleagues in the academic world. The private teacher is restricted to teaching after school and at weekends. This inevitably means that, unless she is prepared to forego some of her income, she has no time to attend any meetings or evening classes that would, if such were available, put her in touch with teachers of other subjects.

There are many laudable attempts to keep instrumental – particularly piano – teachers in touch with *each other*, by means of occasional seminars and workshops. These can be valuable and much appreciated, but it is only comparatively recently that the phenomenon of the dyslexic pupil has been allowed an airing – mostly in the form of unanswered questions – among the weightier subjects of 'the technique required for Scarlatti sonatas or for Debussy's pedalling', and so on. Those nagging questions about dyslexia remain dangling in the air. They are not all easily answered, but there are some solutions, and if we apply what is known of the teaching of dyslexic pupils in other areas – where there has been much success – there is some chance that difficulties will be overcome and progress facilitated.

In recent years, there has been a huge growth in the marketing of electronic keyboards. Schools now timetable lessons for classes in keyboard playing, which is a new and appealing way of learning the basics of musical literacy. The use of the term 'keyboard' in this book is restricted to the non-electronic piano, although I feel sure that there might well be exciting possibilities if a dyslexic pupil were to learn to play the electronic variety.

The incidence of dyslexia among boys and girls is calculated to be anything from 2:1 to 4:1 in favour of boys. Why this should be is as yet an unanswered question and need not concern us here, but it is the reason why I have chosen to classify the dyslexic pupil as 'he' and, for clarity's sake, the teacher as 'she'. No offence intended either to female dyslexic pupils or male teachers!

There is a glossary of both dyslexia-related and music terms at the end of this book.

Chapter 1
Recognizing dyslexia – the way forward

Is there any point in trying to teach a dyslexic pupil to play a musical instrument? What strategies will be involved that we do not already employ in normal teaching? How can we avoid the whole experience ending in failure for both the pupil and the teacher? This book is an attempt to answer those questions and to suggest that, for anyone interested in the art of teaching, to teach a dyslexic pupil can be a journey of exploration that is richly rewarding. It is a journey that the teacher and the pupil make together, neither knowing where it will lead. Nor should there be any assumption that low expectations are to be an accepted element if one takes on a dyslexic pupil. Often, quite the reverse is the case. The teacher may start out with a vision of what may happen, as may the pupil to a limited extent, but, as in most of life, the unexpected always lies around the corner.

'Since music is a language with some meaning at least for the immense majority of mankind, although only a tiny minority of people are capable of formulating a meaning in it, and since it is the only language with the contributory attributes of being at once intelligible and untranslatable, the musical creator is a being comparable to the gods, and music itself the supreme mystery of the science of man' (Lévi-Strauss, 1964). The anthropologist Lévi-Strauss is not alone among scientists in claiming that, if we can explain music, we may find the key for all of human thought – or in implying that failure to take music seriously weakens any account of the human condition (Gardner, 1983.). The language of music is one that every child has a right to learn and which every musician, performer or teacher – particularly teacher – must pass on to the next generation. The doors must be opened to everyone who wishes to walk in.

Dyslexia–preliminary thoughts

The Introduction to the Code of Practice on the Identification and Assessment of Special Educational Needs (issued by the Secretary of State for Education in response to a requirement in the 1993 Education Act) begins 'To enable pupils with special educational needs to benefit *as fully as possible* from their education presents teachers, and all the professionals and administrators involved, with some of the most *challenging* and *rewarding* work the education service can offer' (The italics are mine). Further on in the Code (p. 56), there is the heading 'Specific Learning Difficulties (for example Dyslexia)'. Not only is it our pleasure and our privilege to take on dyslexic pupils, but it could also be argued that it is beholden on us to do so.

There are few accomplishments outside the world of sport that require no literary skills at all. Where music is concerned, I believe that we teachers in general have regarded a persistent inability to read music as an inescapable bar to success in the profession, even when it has been obvious that the pupil was musical, and we have ultimately abandoned the musically illiterate to their fate. There are many excellent musicians in the world of popular music, in which an ability to read music is inessential. Success in their world primarily depends upon aural ability; musical literacy, although it may be much valued, comes second. I am afraid that there must be many people, some of them innately musical, who regard themselves as failures in the field because they never learnt to read or to perform even elementary music competently. We teachers have not had the energy, imagination or curiosity to find out why our proven methods of teaching have not produced for the pupil the expected results. In reality, the failure has so often been ours.

Dyslexia (*dys* = Greek for poor or hard, *lexia* = Greek for language) is much more than difficulty with words; its repercussions may be recognized right across the teaching spectrum. The common denominator for all music is sound – that which our ears hear and translate into something meaningful. Second to that is the score – that which our eyes perceive. Pictures are sent to the brain, which in turn sends messages to the muscles telling them how to act. These two aspects – sound and sight – are two of the primary areas in which dyslexics have difficulty; therefore much of what is under consideration will have significance for all music teachers. There are secondary areas – left/right confusion, physical control, memory problems, distractability, lack of self-esteem and disorganization – the consideration of which is not restricted to piano teaching alone.

Some of these secondary areas – notably left/right confusion – may be considered to be more important for some students than are the widely recognized primary areas. It is not unknown for a dyslexic musician to have no particular problem with reading the score but to get into a dreadful tangle when it comes to deciding which hand has to play or to crossing the hands on the keyboard. Everything depends on the nature and the severity of the difficulties that each pupil has.

Dyslexia in greater detail

In the Code of Practice mentioned above, there is a brief guideline setting out what, in the Department for Education's estimation, dyslexia is:

'Some children may have significant difficulties in reading, writing, spelling or manipulating numbers, which are not typical of their general level of performance. They may gain some skills in some subjects quickly and demonstrate a high level of ability orally, yet may encounter sustained difficulty in gaining literacy or numeracy skills. Such children can become severely frustrated and may also have emotional and/or behavioural difficulties.'

This is a good general description of an anomaly in the field of learning that may be encountered by some children. It leaves room for a fairly wide interpretation of the effect that dyslexia may have on the child, and it does not attempt to define the cause.

There have been many definitions of what has come to be known as dyslexia. Some say that it is incapable of being defined. Unfortunately, there is still no universally acceptable definition, but there is a clear distinction between acquired dyslexia and developmental dyslexia. Acquired dyslexia is the condition engendered by a stroke, or something similar, which renders the patient unable to manipulate words. Developmental dyslexia is probably genetically determined (Galaburda et al., 1994); it is a specific learning difficulty. It is with developmental dyslexia that we are concerned in this book.

As we explore language-based phenomena with ever-increasingly sophisticated machinery and methods of research, so we observe that the percentage of those having trouble increases. It has been calculated that there are now anything up to 40 different subtraits of dyslexia, which adds credence to the critics' claims. Frank Duffy, Associate Professor of Neurology, Harvard Medical School, Boston, Massachusetts, USA, believes that the term dyslexia should not be used as being synonymous with Specific Learning Difficulties as there are many non-language-based learning difficulties. It is a source of surprise that educationalists should have for so long considered dyslexia only in relation to reading, writing and spelling. More recently, it has been recognized in the field of mathematics (dyscalculia), completing the trio of the three Rs, but the cognitive effect that it has on many other fields has only lately begun to be widely acknowledged. There are many schools of thought on the subject. Research, into both the causes of specific learning difficulties and their remediation, continues to be carried out all over the world. It is not a purely Western phenomenon nor concerned exclusively with the English language. It does exist, and the fact that at last it has official recognition in the world of education, at least in Great Britain, is testimony to this proposition, even if the term should be considered to be an umbrella term for a pattern of difficulties.

Some researchers have reached the conclusion that dyslexics' brains differ from non-dyslexics' brains (Galaburda et al., 1994). It is not my intention here to attempt to explain how they differ – there are many books and papers on the subject – but simply to set out the symptoms of these differences. How they will apply more specifically to music will be considered in Chapters 3–8.

The crucial clause in the guideline for the identification of a dyslexic, quoted above, is 'which are not typical of their general level of performance'. A child with dyslexia who is perhaps 2, 3 or more years *behind* expectations for his chronological age in reading and spelling may yet be articulate and capable of reasoning in a manner well *in advance* of his chronological age. This, in itself, creates difficulties that are secondary to the condition of dyslexia, although psychologically they may be of equal importance.

It should be emphasized that not all the difficulties listed below are necessarily found in every dyslexic; for example, those who have visual problems often have excellent aural recall. Nor will everyone agree with the order in which I have compiled the list. I do not wish to give particular prominence to any one feature, merely to set out a handy checklist in which the music teacher may recognize a persistent problem, or problems, that her pupil may be having. It should also be understood that, in the absence of a universally accepted definition of dyslexia, it would be inappropriate to claim that the following symptoms are symptoms of dyslexia itself. They merely give rise to one or more of the learning difficulties that might signify the presence of dyslexia. So do not despair! Seen in this light, the following list will not seem nearly so daunting.

Primary symptoms

Auditory (language-based)

1.   Slowness in processing what is heard. This applies to speech as well as to, particularly, rhythm. Prosody (the musical element of speech) and musical rhythm are controlled by the left hemisphere in the brain in 'normal' right-handers, whereas pitch and tonality in singing (but not in speech) are controlled by the right hemisphere. 'Almost any musical performance is therefore dependent upon perfect hemispherical coordination' (Borch-grevink, 1982). If the two ears are not hearing at the same speed, this will not be possible.
2.   Inability to recognize rhyme.
3.   Inability to recognize and manipulate sound segmentation and sound blend-ing, which, together with the inability to recognize rhyme, results in poor spelling and reading. Words written on a page of music to help a beginner are, for the most part, a waste of time. The learning of Italian terms is hard. Unless they are already in the dyslexic pupil's long-term memory, words to accompany short tunes seldom help general performance.

Visual

1.   An inability to maintain a fixed focus (unstable binocular control). This is the result of lack of dominance of one eye or the other. We all have a domi-nant eye if we are normally fortunate. Try looking through a tube as if it were a telescope. You will automatically raise the tube to your dominant eye. The dyslexic with unstable binocular control may effectively switch from eye to eye, giving him the impression that what he is trying to focus on is moving from left to right or vice versa. Accuracy of interpretation of the text is therefore considerably at risk.
2.   An inability to maintain steady directional progress. This can result in both omissions and insertions, as well as the place being lost altogether owing to the eyes having skipped a word (musicians read 'beat' or 'group of notes', etc.). The eyes may regress to something already read or even slip up or down to the preceding or following line.

3. Susceptibility to glare and the effect that stripes (notably the stave) can have.
4. Lack of competence in recognition of similarities and differences in the text. This is as much to do with visual memory (see Chapter 6).

Spatial

1. Confusion between left and right. The dyslexic is often unaware of the midline between the two complementary sides of his body. This results in difficulties with deciding which hand is required to play. When it is necessary for the two hands to cross over each other, there is considerable disorientation. He often finds beating time confusing. General clumsiness is sometimes apparent.
2. An inability to judge distance. This will be noticed in the early stages of learning to play an instrument by his spatial relationship to it. He will sit too close, or too far away and his fine motor skills (writing and the manipulation of his fingers) may also be impaired. The vertical correlation on the page between the notes to be played by the right hand and those to be played by the left is especially difficult for him. Sometimes he will not have a ready understanding of up/down or high/low. When theoretical work has to be done, he may find it very hard to be accurate and tidy.

Memory

Both visual and auditory memory can be deficient in the short term. The converse of this is that once something has been committed to the long-term memory, it is almost impossible to erase it!

Disorganization

Dyslexics are notorious for their disorganization. It has been observed that they often have an impaired sense of time passing, as if their difficulties with sequencing spilled over into everyday life. They find it difficult to organize themselves, their equipment and also their method of work. They need particular help with practising, which demands skills in all these areas. They find it difficult to order such things as key signatures correctly and are unlikely to recognize sequences.

Secondary symptoms

Poor concentration

This can often be because the child is unsure of on what he is supposed to be concentrating. If his eyes are playing tricks on him and the messages that his ears are receiving are coming too fast for him to process properly, it is hardly surprising that his brain gives up.

Poor copying skills

There can be an inability to retain in his visual memory that which has to be copied, making theoretical work slow and laborious.

Anxiety

This is particularly noticeable because the dyslexic child is often acutely aware of his shortcomings. Where music is concerned, he can be particularly worried about 'making mistakes' because, as music essentially exists in time, these cannot be erased.

Low self-esteem

This is a very important and sometimes inevitable result of having to face the fact that his peers are bounding ahead academically while he is still metaphorically crawling. A confident musician will handle phrasing, dynamics, rhythm and articulation with style. He will also keep going even if he does make a notational mistake, but lack of confidence produces a faltering and flat performance.

Frustration

In the face of his debilitating difficulties, the intelligent dyslexic may give way to sheer frustration. He knows that he is not stupid, but he is unable to access those parts of his brain that he needs.

Family problems

The dyslexic is not always an easy person to live with: he can drive others to exasperation! This occasionally means that he does not receive the help he deserves. On the other hand, I must say that I have more frequently come across extemely supportive and understanding parents who have been prepared to help with their child's practising. Some can go *too* far and visit their own anxiety about their offspring on the child himself. The middle road is an uneasy balance to maintain.

Erratic behaviour

This is sometimes the most difficult aspect of dyslexia. One day a dyslexic may be able to perform well, whereas the next day the identical task may be almost impossible for him. Practical examinations (see Chapter 8) are therefore a big risk. Much will depend upon his equilibrium: stressful circumstances can unbalance his performance, as can poor health.

The positive angle

All the negative symptoms above might well induce one to think that any attempt by a dyslexic at learning to play a musical instrument would be doomed to failure. How can we then explain the presence of dyslexic musicians – both students and professors – in colleges and academies of music throughout the land? It is not only a tribute to some excellent, sympathetic teaching, but it is also very largely due to the indefatigable courage and resolution of the dyslexic musicians themselves. It is a phenomenon of many dyslexics that they never give up. The fact that they face difficulties in many areas seems to breed in some of them a superhuman determination to succeed. This is a splendidly positive attitude to life, which those of us who have had an altogether easier time of it might do well to emulate.

Another positive symptom of dyslexia, arising like a phoenix from the ashes, is a compensatory ingeniousness. Where normal, well-tried methods fail, the dyslexic pupil will quite often find his own way round the problem. That is one of the great delights of teaching them. When Ben simply could not understand that notes going up on the page meant that they were going higher and therefore to the right on the keyboard, although he could *hear* the difference, his teacher said to him, 'What are we going to do about this Ben?' Ben thought for a moment and then said, 'Well, you could draw a line on the piano going up like this' – indicating a line sloping up towards the treble. They compromised by sticking a yellow 'post-it' label high up on the treble end and a blue one low down, close to the keyboard in the bass. His teacher wrote 'Up. High' and 'Down. Low'. The problem was solved – by Ben himself.

One teacher said to me, 'I don't understand how his mind works, but he seems to find a way of getting there in the end.' This seems to put the situation in a nutshell. It is all too easy to dwell on the difficulties because they are evident, but each dyslexic learns to compensate for his own particular weaknesses. He seems to have an instinct for survival, and with encouragement his inventiveness flourishes. Another teacher quoted the old saying 'Once you know what the problem is, it ceases to be a problem'.

There are many experts in the field of dyslexia who agree that, with early intervention, the right kind of teaching, support from everyone involved and determination, the intelligent dyslexic pupil will eventually learn the basic literary skills that will see him through adult life. There is a suggestion (Hornsby, 1988) that the cells of a young (0–5 years) child's brain are capable of adapting and changing. As he grows older, the propensity for change lessens, but the pathways into understanding and memory are incalculably many and the dyslexic sometimes gets to know himself so well that he can accept what we would call his disability with cheerfulness. An ex-pupil said, 'I know me now, and I wouldn't have me any different. I rather enjoy it !'

Herbert Lubs, Professor of Paediatrics, University of Miami, Florida, USA, studied over 100 families with dyslexics over three generations during the 1970s and 1980s. He hypothesized that there were biological *advantages* to the presence of dyslexia in these families because so many of them were unusually creative or productive; there *is* a bright side to the picture.

Where to get help

When a pupil is failing at basic literary skills at school for no apparent reason, being of average-to-good intelligence, as measured by his thoughtful oral replies, and in good health, he should soon come to the notice of his teachers. An application can be made to have him assessed by a professional from outside the school, and, according to this assessment, remedial teaching can be arranged for him within the school. Parents sometimes prefer to organize their own assessments and remedial help. Whatever happens, the first real step in the right direction is the professional assessment.

Professionals have varying methods of assessment, but in general terms they are all approaching the task in the same way. They may want to know:

1.   what his developmental history has been – this is in order to check that there are no congenital factors that may be affecting his academic performance;
2.   what his schooling has been – a child who has had to make many changes of school and who has been the subject of several different teaching methods may have fallen behind for this reason;
3.   what his school reports say about him;
4.   what his general level of functioning is – this can take the form of several different kinds of intelligence test, both verbal and non-verbal. It will also test his ability to discriminate both visually and aurally, his short-term visual and aural memory, his laterality (whether he is left- or right-handed, eyed, eared or footed), and his general attainment in reading, writing and spelling.

Throughout the tests, the assessor will make very careful notes about the child's attitude – whether he is particularly stressed by any test, if he gets tired easily, which tests he seems to enjoy and his general level of cooperation. The assessor will sometimes give recommendations on what kind of remedial teaching would be of value.

Once the assessment has been made, both the school and the parents will have a much clearer picture of what is wrong and what positive steps can be taken. Knowledge of areas in which the child is having particular difficulty can be of great value to the music teacher. Sometimes, she may only have her own suspicions confirmed – the teacher working with her pupil on a one-to-one basis can get to know him very well – but even this confirmation is a help. If one knows that he has a particular difficulty with short-term visual memory, one will not expect him to remember the shape of a broken chord seen a moment ago. One will be much more wary of challenging his memory. At the same time, one will take extra care to help him to learn the broken chord shape, thinking up all sorts of ways to impress it upon him so that his memory for it becomes more reliable. If tests, administered by somebody whose judgement the teacher has reason to respect, reinforce her individual opinion, the teacher's confidence in herself is reaffirmed and the isolation that she may have felt, when trying to teach a pupil who was not responding in the expected way, is reduced.

The assessment, then, is valuable as a picture of the present situation. It is also valuable for what it may contribute to future strategies. Andrew, aged 7;4 years, was diagnosed as having poor auditory memory and perception. It was suggested by the assessor, among other things, that a story should be audiotaped for him with several mistakes in it and that he should be given the script and encouraged to spot the mistakes. The Associated Board of the Royal Schools of Music aural tests mirror this idea in sound. By inventing much easier tests than these, but along the same lines, his piano teacher had the assurance that she was doing the right thing to help him and that, even if he never excelled at playing the piano, at least she would be helping him towards better literacy.

So the instrumental teacher can turn, with the parents' permission and assistance, to the educational assessment for guidance and help. It goes without saying, I hope, that she will discuss her pupil as freely as possible with the parents: they are the first who should be consulted if there is any difficulty. But what if the pupil has had no assessment? Sometimes, particularly if the child is in a very large class at school, the music teacher is the first person on the scene to notice that there is a problem.

Martin's mother had warned his new teacher that 'Martin is not like other children. He is very musical, but he finds the piano very difficult. He won't give up though.' He had already been having piano lessons for about a year. After a week or two, she began to wonder if his eyesight was bothering him, but it had been tested by the school doctor and found to be normal. The main trouble seemed to be that he kept on losing his place, besides being occasionally unable, apparently, to see whether a note was on a line or in a space. His mother agreed to take him to an ophthalmologist in the holidays and also to have him assessed for dyslexia. Both the dyslexia test and the visit to the ophthalmologist had far-reaching results. He was pronounced 'mildly dyslexic' and the ophthalmologist found that, although each eye had perfect sight, his *eye function* was at fault, i.e. the two eyes were not functioning at the same speed. She was able to give him eye exercises that gradually began to ameliorate the problem, and although he remained mildly dyslexic, he was given the help he needed. Four years later he won a music scholarship.

I quote this as an example of teamwork and as a suggestion that the music teacher is very much part of the team. I have mentioned above (see p. 5) that it can happen that a dyslexic child is unaware of the midline between the two complementary sides of his body. He confuses left and right and does not seem to know where he is, often getting lost in even quite familiar surroundings. This leads to writing letters the wrong way round, using an uneven script – some letters being tiny and others far too big – and misplacing letters when reading and spelling. The piano teacher is obliged constantly to refer to right and left, helping him to establish the concept and also to reinforce this concept with sound. The high sounds on the right, the low ones on the left. This is perhaps an argument for the merits of the piano as a musical instrument to learn: both sides of the body are involved equally. Not only that, but all the fingers have to learn to work equally well and the player has to be aware of which finger he is using. Playing the piano helps him to get to know his own body better (see Chapter 5). It can be the case that the child whose fingerwork on the keyboard improves also makes a marked improvement in his writing. Proof is not positive that this is always the case, but as his fine motor coordination improves in one area, the expectations are that it will improve in another where the same fine skills are involved.

In the world outside the door of the music studio, there are huge numbers of people all busying themselves trying to come up with answers to the question 'Why'? Why has he got dyslexia? Why do there seem to be more dyslexics now than ever before? Why does he find it so hard? What is going on in his brain? What is the best way to help him? So far, very little clinical research has been carried out into the effect that music and instrumental lessons can have on the dyslexic pupil. We have no specific guidelines. I believe that our job as teachers of music is to find out as much as we can about the problem, but to be wary of new ideas until they are thoroughly tested and proven. That is not to say that if some-body suggests a way of helping – 'Try singing into his right ear instead' – we should not experiment and see if it works. No harm can come of this so long as we do not jump to any conclusions or expect that what works for one child will also work for another. All we can do is get on with the job of teaching – of opening doors – as sympathetically and as well as we can, using, as far as we can, the guide-lines that are offered to classroom teachers.

Multisensory teaching

The foremost piece of advice that is given to teachers of dyslexics in the classroom is to teach multisensorily. They are exhorted to employ as many of the child's senses as possible in the hope that stronger senses will compensate for weaker ones and a pathway into the brain and the memory will be found. It is suggested that the child *listens* to a sound, *sees* what it looks like when written down, *feels* what it is like in his mouth, traces it in the air or on a sand tray, perhaps sees what his teeth and tongue and lips do when he makes it, and finally experiences the sensation of writing it down. The principle that is involved here is easily translatable into the world of music. In fact, learning the art of music is in itself a multisensory activity. We use our ears to hear, our eyes to see and our fingers to feel. Music moves through our whole bodies – even our feet are involved. Our eyes see the page or the keyboard, and our ears listen not only to what we *want* to hear but also to what we *do* hear.

The outstanding exponents of the multisensory approach to the teaching of music in the late nineteenth century and the twentieth century have been Émile Jaques-Dalcroze (1865–1950) and Zoltan Kodály (1882–1967). It was through Jaques-Dalcroze's efforts to broaden the basis of musical education that the system of coordinating music with bodily movement, known today as eurythmics, was born. This is practised widely through the Western world and Australia, and continues to have an impact in the world of opera, theatre and drama. Its primary object is 'to create by the help of rhythm a rapid and regular current of communication between brain and body, and to make feeling for rhythm a physical experience' (Jaques-Dalcroze, 1930). Those of us who employ the little stratagem of making our pupils walk around the room in time to crotchets, run in time to quavers and skip to 6/8 time will understand how valuable even such a basic internalizing of rhythm can be. Experience showed Jacques-Dalcroze that 'the child has difficulty in grasping at one and the same time a melodic line and the rhythm that breathes spirit into it' (Jaques-Dalcroze 1965). This is a picture that we will recognize all too easily when teaching dyslexic pupils: many of them find it hard to concentrate on more than one thing at a time. The works of Jaques-Dalcroze make fascinating reading and are highly recommended.

Zoltan Kodály's influence in the teaching world of music was, and continues to be, of great significance. Kodály's philosophy of education evolved in Hungary, but its influence has gradually spread to the rest of the world. Indeed, in his later years, he was honorary president of the International Society for Music Education. He believed 'that true musical literacy – the ability to read, write and think music – is the right of every human being'. It was he who adapted the system of rhythm syllables (time names) from the work of Émile Joseph Chevé to assist in the perception of rhythm. These syllables, – ta, ta-té, etc., can be of real value provided that they are taught from a very early age. Even if they are not, they can sometimes assist in tight corners where the combination of rhythm and pitch are proving too much.

> 'What has made Kodály's ideas so significant in the world of music education? It is just *that*: they are ideas. They are the embodiment of something much larger than a bag of tricks by which to teach.' (Choksy, 1981)

Over the last 30 years, the essence of the ideas of Jaques-Dalcroze and Kodály as well as those of some of the best education practitioners of the past four hundred years, i.e. Comenius, Curwen, Gordon, Orff, Pestalozzi, Steiner and Suzuki, have been fused and augmented by Froseth, whose experiments in music learning research have resulted in the Froseth Method. This method, known as the Comprehensive Music Learning Sequence, is a non-verbal music learning sequence that is divided into three main components containing every basic facet of music learning except historical and theoretical facts. It is for use in the classroom, but many of the ideas and techniques it employs can be adapted for use in the solo lesson. It is a method widely used in the USA and it is rapidly gaining ground in the UK.

Teaching to strengths

Besides making sure that *all* our teaching – technique, aural training, sight reading, theory, learning pieces for performance (even if only in the lesson) and perhaps keyboard harmony and improvising – is as multisensory as possible, it is suggested that we should teach to a dyslexic's strengths. What is meant by this? It is quite simple really, particularly if the parents can tell us before we begin where he scored well in his assessment. It is worth asking. It means that we should capitalize on his best skills, encouraging him to use them so that he has the best possible chance for success. For example, if he has a good aural memory but poor visual skills, he should be allowed to learn and play from memory and not be forced to read the music. That is not to say that he can neglect learning to read music; he will still need this ability when help is not at hand during his practising, and his weaknesses should be strengthened as much as possible. This can be done, however, as a separate exercise. In the meantime, he should be allowed to learn some pieces entirely from memory, perhaps never seeing the written music.

Alternatively, if he has poor motor coordination but good visual ability, great care should be taken in choosing pieces for him which exploit his visual strength but which do not challenge his coordination too much. He will probably enjoy duets in which his own part is simple but the general effect, combined with the teacher's part, is very pleasing. He will feel that he has had a share in creating a real piece of music.

The older student often knows what his own strengths and weaknesses are and is usually quite willing to discuss them. The most difficult pupil to get to know is the one who may have been learning for some time with somebody else and who is unwilling to recognize – perhaps because of parental influence – that he has dyslexia. There is still a prejudice against using the word and admitting to the label, as if there were something discreditable about it. Until the time comes when it is not seen as threatening and shameful, we are bound to meet with this unwillingness. If the student has been learning with someone else who has perhaps concurred with the parents' view either that dyslexia does not exist or that, at least, their child is not dyslexic, it will take a long time to find out how much he really knows and where his strengths and weaknesses lie. If, however, the teacher is alive to what dyslexia is and how best to help, the chances are that the pupil will progress in spite of the parents' misgivings about diagnosis.

Summary

As research both into the brain and into teaching has become increasingly widespread and sophisticated, the weighty arguments in favour of the recognition of Sp L D (Specific Learning Difficulties), also known as dyslexia, are winning the day. Sp L D still evades precise definition because there are so many ways in which it can manifest itself, but the crucial element in diagnosis is the discrepancy between the intelligence of the child and his performance in literacy-related skills. Many years ago, music may not have been judged one of these skills, but it is a many-faceted art requiring visual, aural and kinetic competence, all of which may be impaired in the dyslexic. Music is now part of the national curriculum in the UK.

There are both primary and secondary symptoms of dyslexia. The primary symptoms are in the language-based, visual, spatial, memory and organizational fields. The secondary symptoms are the result of the primaries and reveal themselves in poor concentration, poor copying skills, anxiety, low self-esteem, frustration, possible family problems and erratic behaviour. There is, however, another side to the coin: dyslexics can be determined, ingenious, inventive and creative. They learn at an early age to develop their talents to the full and never to give up.

The music teacher is part of a team of people who are all concerned with the welfare of the pupil. Other professionals are employed to give general assessments or diagnoses, and at all times the parents are the vital link between the child, the school, the professionals who have been consulted and the teacher. There is no need for the teacher to feel isolated, and it is well worth her while making her presence in that team felt. In her privileged position of one-to-one weekly contact with her pupil, she can often make observations that may be missed by others.

The best advice that an instrumental teacher can follow is that which is given to all teachers of dyslexics in the classroom: teach multisensorily and teach to the pupil's strengths. Music is ideally suited for this. I shall hope to show in some detail how these principles can be applied.

Chapter 2
Communication — the pupil and the teacher

Music is part of every human being. It is woven into the very fabric of our lives. Long before the written word, music united people in song and dance, and it has always had the power to excite and to calm, to inspire, to frighten, to lift the spirits and to gladden the heart. Why is music so powerful? Because music is a language and language is a means of communication. 'The origins of music may be lost in obscurity but, from its earliest beginnings, it seems to have played an essential part in social interaction' (Storr, 1992).

Music as communication

When children start having music lessons, there will probably be no grandiose ideas of learning to communicate with their fellow men in their minds. It is more likely that they will be fascinated by the way musicians' fingers move so fast and produce such exciting or moving tunes. They will know, although the knowledge may not yet have been voiced, that they love particular types of sound and that one piece of music may make them feel happy whereas another may make them feel sad or melancholy. They will want to have the power to recreate these feelings for themselves. Quite soon, they begin to realize that other people react in the same way as they do and that in and through music they can be, and already are, part of a thinking, feeling, reacting community. It gives them a consciousness of belonging to a new and very exciting world.

On the other hand, written language as a means of communication is a concept with which the dyslexic child already has difficulty: 'By about 7 or so, the child has barely made a start in reading and spelling, and has become demotivated' (Thomson, 1990). The universal language of music offers a new way of communicating that can break down the barriers of isolation and lead the child into a rich and absorbing world where he can have freedom and power. It can remotivate him. We, as musicians and teachers, have the opportunity to assist in breaking down those barriers and opening doors. Percy Buck, the first lecturer on Psychology at the Royal College of Music in London, even went so far as to say to students, 'You and I know how great music can open the windows of heaven; and you must realize that, to the majority of your pupils, the only possibility of ever getting a glimpse into Paradise depends on you.'

With these awesome but very real possibilities on the doorstep, how are we best going to respond?

When teaching any pupil, one does one's best to get to know something about his likes and dislikes, his family background and what he likes to do outside school hours. Having a chat about things unconnected with school and lessons helps to create a bond of friendship and a positive relationship conducive to willing cooperation and, therefore, one hopes, good progress. It is not going to be easy to form that bond with a demotivated child unless one has much more information about the kind of experiences that he will have had up to the present time.

What has happened? He has been labelled 'dyslexic', but you and I know that labels can be dangerous: they tend to classify without leaving room for individuality. They can be useful, and in this case they are, but the music teacher meeting a diagnosed dyslexic for the first time needs, if possible, to have not only a knowledge of what the term dyslexia may mean (this has been briefly explored in Chapter 1), but also a much clearer picture of the psychological effect that not only the label, but also, probably more importantly, the circumstances leading to the diagnosis may, or may not, have had.

The diagnosed dyslexic child

In the UK, children with learning difficulties are not usually brought to the notice of professionals in child educational psychology or qualified assessors until they are at least 7 years old. In other countries, notably Australia, they can be identified earlier, and programmes to help them can be instigated at the age of 6. Signs that there may be difficulties of a dyslexic nature are often undoubtedly present from a very early age, so it is for this reason that the assessors need to know the whole history of the child. They will be looking for a possible family history of dyslexia or anything in his medical history that might have resulted in dyslexic tendencies being exacerbated. They will also be noting any character trait that might have developed; they can sometimes make positive suggestions that can help to alleviate difficult situations.

The case of Andrew

Andrew's mother is herself dyslexic, having particular problems with laterality. Her pregnancy was fraught with difficulties of all kinds, but the baby survived and Andrew was born quite normally.

At 1 year old, Andrew had a short spell in hospital suffering from gastroenteritis, and when he was 4 years old he had an adenoidectomy during which his ears were drilled and drained. His sleeping pattern throughout these first 4 years was very irregular, creating very tired parents, who by this time had a daughter as well, Andrew being the first child. He suffered continually from enuresis and had distressing bouts of hayfever in the summer months.

Andrew was a very active baby but he never crawled, and when he began to walk he continued to fall over a great deal more than most toddlers. When he began speaking shortly after he was 2 years old, his speech was very unclear, and even at the age of 8 he was still having trouble with vowel sounds. By this time, his reading was 3 years behind for his age, his spelling was bizarre and he had developed an aversion to writing anything at all because the effort and concentration were too much for him.

It was when Andrew reached this stage, a few months before his 9th birthday, that he was assessed by an educational psychologist and found to have difficulties in many areas – visual, aural and spatial – and with poor short-term memory.

Andrew was a boy of *average intelligence*, but during his early schooling he had gradually begun to form a picture of himself that was far from the truth. His frustration at not being able to keep up with his peers' literary skills, and the comments that had been made by them and, regretfully, by some of his teachers, had occasionally led to violence. He was teased and bullied. He had begun to think of himself as not only stupid and lazy but 'bad' as well. He was very disorganized and at times depressed, but beneath it all lay an affectionate, fun-loving character. The activity he enjoyed most at school was music. He particularly loved singing and developed a close relationship with the music teacher, who then unfortunately left.

For some time after being told that he was dyslexic, Andrew demonstrably felt that if he were stupid *and* dyslexic too, there was not much point in trying. He would not believe that he had no less than average intelligence. He lost what little motivation he had, and it was well over a year before sympathetic teaching and understanding gradually began to help him to readjust the picture he had of himself.

The case of Philip

Philip was also the first child in the family. There were no pre-birth difficulties, but when he was born he suffered jaundice for 3 weeks, for which he was eventually given phototherapy treatment. He inherited an allergy to cows milk from his mother, and suffered from constant constipation while he was a toddler until he was taken off all dairy products. He also had mild asthma and frequent ear infections.

Philip's speech developed very slowly, and when he was 3 years old, he began a year of having speech therapy sessions. He was, however, quite an active child and crawled and walked quite normally. He enjoyed creative play and was particularly good at constructing things with Lego. He showed no interest in books or nursery rhymes, although his parents bought tapes and played them in the car to encourage him to learn them.

When Philip started at primary school, aged almost 5, he made many friends. He had an engaging personality and was good at football. Slowly, however, things began to go wrong. He appeared to be intelligent but he was slow at learning to read and his writing and spelling were atrocious. He started saying to his parents, 'I'm useless'. By the time he was 7 years old, he was well behind the others in his class, and his sunny personality was gradually disappearing. He began to be very difficult at home, and the slightest thing seemed to upset him and make him cry. His parents felt that a barrier was developing between them and their son that they did not understand.

An assessment was arranged for Philip and it was found that he was of *moderately high intelligence* but that his auditory skills were poor and he found any form of sequencing very difficult. He was therefore performing well below what one would expect for a boy of his age and general underlying ability. When he was told that he had dyslexia, he immediately wanted to know what it meant. His father realized that he too had been and still was dyslexic, although when he was at school he had never heard of dyslexia. He was now succeeding as a teacher of metalwork in a technical college. Philip's parents managed to persuade him that with his intelligence and with plenty of determination there was no reason why he too should not succeed and that, now that they and all his teachers understood what his difficulties were, he would be gradually able to overcome them.

The common denominator

The character trait that both these children had developed by the age of 7½ to 8 was a lack of faith in themselves. This is so common among dyslexics. Over and over again, one hears of a case in which the child self-esteem has reached such a low level as to be almost non-existent. They are badly lacking in confidence and often very sensitive, being conscious of the expectations that their teachers and their families have for them and their consistent failure to meet those expectations.

The undiagnosed child

Unfortunately, there are children who slip through the net for some reason or other, perhaps illness or frequent changes of school, without ever having been assessed for dyslexia. Their parents may be loth to admit either to themselves or to their offspring that a dyslexia problem may exist. These parents also sometimes arrange music lessons for their children. They often hope that a teacher will not notice, or that there will be something about learning to play an instrument, like having the sole attention of a teacher, that will make their child learn to concentrate. They may feel that concentration is merely a matter of willpower and that their child will be obliged to learn to concentrate under such conditions. They foresee the benefit of this being reflected in the classroom. These are the people who are not going, as they see it, to jeopardize their child's chances of success by alerting the teacher to the possibility of trouble ahead. It is left to the teacher to find out.

I now recognize that, in the past, I have probably taught several pupils without ever realizing that they had some form of dyslexia, the possibility never having been mentioned to me by the parents or anyone else. I am not blaming the parents – they probably did not know themselves, although they may have suspected something of the kind. They may not have realized what it entailed when it came to reading or playing music. Nor would I have known myself what dyslexia was and how best to teach a dyslexic. I have persevered with some pupils for months, and even years, using mnemonics for the lines of the staves – my mnemonics or theirs, whichever they wanted – and inventing stories using words with the letters A to G, either for them to decipher from the written music or for them to write as notes on the page. I have tried to get them to feel for the keys while keeping their eyes on the music ahead. I have used all the tricks of the trade as I know it, down to outright bribery, to try and engender some understanding and improvement. Eventually, I have recommended to the parents that they give up having piano lessons and try taking up a different instrument, or give up altogether. I am fairly sure that many a piano teacher will recognize the scenario.

How should I have known that they were dyslexic?

There are many telltale characteristics, several of which have already been discussed in Chapter 1. Let us consider them now as they relate to music and the music pupil.

The first thing that one is likely to notice about a dyslexic pupil is that he is confused about left and right. In technical terms he may be a crossed lateral (see p. 30), preferring, for example, to use his left hand but his right eye, or he may show inconsistencies in his use of hand or eye, resulting in mixed laterality. The notion of laterality and its association with dyslexia is a contentious one (Thomson, 1990). Much research has been done on the subject, but Thomson concludes, 'It is difficult to see how left/right confusion per se is linked to inconsistent laterality, but there do appear to be suggestions of difficulties in verbal labelling and information processing, which are key features of the cognitive weakness in dyslexia.'

I often ask my new pupils whether they are left or right handed: I expect other teachers do too. One needs to know from the start which hand they prefer to use. Sometimes a child does not appear to be sure, so I ask which hand he uses to hold his pencil. If he wavers or says 'left' and holds up his right it does not take much observation to realize that he is confused. This confusion may have far-reaching consequences (see Chapter 5). By the age of 8, a child should be able to differentiate between right and left with ease; if he cannot, it is likely that he has a more deep-seated problem, related to dyslexia.

Most instrumental teachers either supply or expect their pupils to supply a notebook in which is written what is to be practised each week. I will be making a few suggestions about this in Chapter 7, but at the first lesson what I have found, ever since I discovered that a child for whom I had been busily writing instructions could not read a word of what I had written, is that it is worth making him read back to you what you have written. You can always say, 'I don't know if you find handwriting easy to read – can you tell me what I have written?' If he can't, you may well begin to suspect that all is not as it should be. It is important, of course, that you make a point of getting him to read the words rather than giving him the opportunity to say 'Yes' and hide from you the fact that he cannot read. He will be good at hiding uncomfortable inabilities by the time he is 8 or more. If there is a reading problem, you can always suggest that it does not matter too much – after all, music is sound, not hieroglyphics on a page – but you will need to make a mental note that writing in his notebook, at any rate for *him* to read, is a waste of time.

If you have invited your new pupil to write his own name on the notebook, you may notice either that he has misspelt it or that his writing is particularly untidy. Either of these should alert you to the possibility of dyslexia being present. Untidiness may range from a marked inconsistency in letter size or spacing, a mixed use of upper and lower case (capitals and small) letters, an inability to keep on a straight line or actual malformation of letters. It is possible also that he may take a very long time over it – trying his best to do it well – and he may be using a very tight 'fist' grip on the pencil or pen.

You may be one of those teachers who introduce the names of the notes on the keyboard at the first lesson, carefully explaining that – starting at the bottom end of the piano – they correspond with the letters of the alphabet, but that when you get to G you have to start again with an A. Even a dyslexic can usually manage this by the age of 8, but what happens if you start at G and descend? Two things:

1. He may be confused about the terminology (ascend, descend, up, down).
2. He will probably be completely unable to work out the letters A to G in reverse order, even if you 'chunk' them for him, for example GFED–CBA or GFE–DCB–A.

There will be more about both of these problems in Chapter 3. Suffice it to say here that either of them should alert you to the possibility of the child being to some extent dyslexic.

There comes a time, usually very near the beginning of learning to read music, when the stave is introduced and it is explained that notes on the stave correspond to keys on the piano: line, space, line, space, etc. Again, there will be much more about this later on (Chapter 4). Alarm bells really should begin to ring if the pupil has difficulty in deciding whether the written note is on a line or in a space. If he has to peer closely at the music in order to decide where the note is, one's immediate reaction is to query whether or not his eyesight is normal. You ask him if he ever has to wear glasses in class, and when the answer 'No' comes back, you make a mental note to mention it to his parents. It is quite likely that his eyesight has already been checked by the school in the normal course of events and it has been passed as perfectly normal, but what has possibly not been checked is how the eyes function together. An abnormality here could give rise to serious consequences, and it is advisable to bear in mind that his eyes could be playing tricks on him that would give rise to symptoms of dyslexia.

Towards the end of the first lesson, I think most of us tend to do a bit of swift revision to make sure that the new pupil understands what has happened and remembers what and how he is going to practise for the following week. Here is where you find out what sort of memory he has, be it auditory, visual or tactile. This is a very cursory understanding of what we call memory and assumes that we expect memory to be a store of everything we have ever learnt and that all we have to do is to fish out the bit we want at the appropriate moment. This is discussed in more detail in Chapter 6.

If the new pupil is dyslexic, you may well find during the quick résumé of the salient points that you want him to remember that he has forgotten them already. You may put this down to the fact that everything is new and perhaps you have told him too much in the first lesson, but you will inevitably think to yourself after he has gone 'This is going to be uphill work'. If you are surprised that he did not appear to have taken in what you said, and yet when you said it he appeared to have understood perfectly, you again have a situation that might be a pointer to the presence of dyslexia.

The dyslexic child is often very disorganized. A problem with organization is not usually apparent at a child's first lesson – a parent has usually seen to that, or if he is having lessons at school, his teacher will probably have sent him along at the right time and he will not at that stage have any particular books to bring with him but, as the weeks go by, it will become more and more obvious. At school, he will be expected, after the first lesson, to remember when and where to come by himself. He may not. Sometimes he will be unaware of the time; sometimes he will not know what day of the week it is; sometimes he will know what day of the week it is but he will think his lesson should be on a different day. He will have any number of excuses. You may have given him a primer, perhaps a book of technical exercises in addition to his notebook and possibly some theory worksheets or a small manuscript book. He will inevitably have left at least one of these behind at his last lesson, unless you have packed them into his case for him, and somehow during the week something will have escaped again. Sometimes the whole case will have gone missing.

Organizing parents in the background are such a help when it comes to having all the right things at the right time, but even they cannot disguise the fact that their child is disorganized. He may come into the room, put all his books on the table or, more usually, the floor and seat himself on the piano stool without having given you his notebook or got his music ready to play. He then has to get off his stool again and rustle about in his case unless you catch him in time and do it all for him. He may have other things with him bulging out of his pockets, and if he has got a handkerchief half a dozen other bits and pieces will fall out when he uses it, whereupon he hops off the stool again and picks them all up, stuffing them back into his pocket on top of his hanky so that they all fall out again next time too.

Many children, dyslexic or not, are disorganized. Sometimes this disorganization only manifests itself in a general feeling of anxiety: the child thinks that he has forgotten to bring something to the lesson or is worried that he may forget to do something that he has been asked to do. One becomes aware that he is apprehensive that something has gone or will go wrong. We all know the small boy who has not done his practising because he went to stay with a friend at the weekend and he left his music there, or whose practice has been missed because he had forgotten to feed the rabbit, but it is when disorganization runs riot and is a positive hindrance to the smooth progress of lessons that we should begin to take note.

The accusation that will have been levelled at the majority of dyslexics at one time or another will be that they are lazy. If one imagines how one would react to being required to struggle with a page of Arabic for half an hour, when one was only capable of recognizing a small number of isolated symbols, one might perhaps begin to understand something of what it is like to be dyslexic. The onslaught from teachers will seem never-ending; by the time he is 7 or 8, the dyslexic will have had 2 or 3 years of sitting in the classroom, yet his reading age may still be that of a 5-year-old. For him, the printed page is baffling and therefore very tiring. Little wonder that he will sometimes use any ruse he can think of to avoid having to battle with it!

Often, however, he clearly needs time and space to recharge his batteries. He needs a rest from what – for him – is much harder work than it is for his peers. He may have been trying twice as hard as they have, with little or nothing to show for it. It is then that the sting of the word 'lazy' really hurts.

It is sometimes difficult to judge whether a pupil is being lazy or whether he has a genuine problem that is preventing him from knowing how to practise on his own, or even from being able to react to what is being asked of him in the lesson. It is very important for the teacher to be absolutely convinced that there is no question of real difficulty before, even in her own mind, she accuses him of not working hard enough. Only he really knows how hard he has been trying. He cannot work hard if he cannot remember exactly what he is supposed to be working at, or if the problem that needs solving has not been clearly delineated. If he *is* dyslexic, not just too interested in something else to be bothered with practising properly, he may need kindly and imaginative help with a difficult passage in a piece for many weeks before he is capable of being able to practise it on his own. A pupil may go away from a lesson saying that he understands what to do, and *at that moment* he may indeed understand, but by the time he gets to the keyboard again his understanding may have evaporated. What is he to do? One thing is certain, which is that he must have confidence that his teacher will sympathize with him in his predicament.

We have already established that by the age of 8+ a dyslexic child may have little, if any, self-esteem. He may have begun to believe that what his teachers and peers have said about him for the last 2 or 3 years is probably right, especially as he has this thing called dyslexia; or perhaps he has gone to the other extreme and decided that, come what may, he is going to prove to the world that he is not stupid and lazy and that he is an achiever after all. However his condition has affected him, we know for certain that he is going to be in a very vulnerable state. This is quite often demonstrated almost immediately when he gets his first bit of praise. This could be when you get him to place his hand on the keyboard in the correct position, or when you invite him to sing or to explain to you what he sees in the innards of the piano when you – or he – depresses a key. Every teacher has her favourite way of getting things going in the first lesson. Some children accept that they are going to get it right from the start, whilst others are much more diffident and positively glow with pride when you say 'Good, well done!' Obviously, it is not this alone that is going to make you think that he does not have much confidence, but his attitude towards success as the lesson progresses is one that should be noted. Of course everyone enjoys praise but there is a subtle difference between someone enjoying praise because he feels that he deserves it and somebody enjoying praise because he is not accustomed to getting it. I am not talking about the child who lives in an emotionally deprived environment *per se*, but about the child who has seen others praised and who has *felt* deprived. This is the child whose reaction to praise is almost one of disbelief.

So there are several clues to the possibility that the child has dyslexia, varying in significance from the more obvious symptoms – inability to read and write, confusion about left and right, difficulty with sequencing, visual disorder and poor memory – down to the subtler symptoms of low self-esteem and bad organization. I have not mentioned awkward hands and stiff fingers because, although these can be a problem – dyslexics often have poor fine motor skills – they can also occur in other children, so it is a common complaint and would not necessarily point, in the first few lessons, to dyslexia. Other children can, and do, have many of the problems I have listed to a small degree without being dyslexic. It is the clear and persistent presence of one or more of these problems, coupled with what appears to be at least average intelligence, that should make you wonder whether he is an undiagnosed dyslexic.

Whether information has been volunteered about the pupil's dyslexia, or has been gleaned from the symptoms displayed in the course of the first few lessons, the teacher has a responsibility to ask herself whether she is the right person to be teaching this child. It is probably safe to assume that anybody reading this book *is* the right person, but it is a task not to be undertaken lightly.

The teacher

The roads leading into the teaching profession are many and varied, and as yet, in England, there is no law that forbids anyone without a teaching degree or diploma from launching out as a teacher of music. Those teaching in most schools will have to be qualified in some way, but we are also talking here about the teacher who teaches from home and who is not employed by any school.

Parents will often choose a teacher for their child for a variety of reasons quite unconnected with whether or not that particular teacher is the best person for their child. Sometimes it is a question of finance, sometimes it is for ease of transport to and from the lesson. It may even be because the teacher is prepared to come to their house or because the teacher can fit the child in at a convenient time.

In order to qualify for an instrumental teaching diploma, we, unlike class music teachers, are not obliged to have done even the most elementary of educational psychology courses. It is possible for somebody with no knowledge of how a young child, teenager or even a young adult may react to varying circumstances to be teaching just such students all day long. We may have forgotten what our own young days were like, and we may have no grounding in psychology to remind us. This, especially when the pupil is dyslexic, is a dangerous scenario.

Our pupils depend on us for every encouragement. The probabilities are that the dyslexic pupil is not going to become a famous concert pianist. It is perhaps worth asking ourselves what proportion of our *non*-dyslexic pupils have become professional musicians. However, if he has enough talent, he may be able to make his living through music in some way or other. There are many niches in the profession, not a few of them filled by dyslexic musicians. We have to be honest with our pupils – nobody would deny this – but not brutally honest. One dyslexic music student has written, in answer to the question 'Have your teachers been sympathetic?', 'Teachers who are aware and knologable are very supportive but others cause emence Embarecment'.

Whichever road has led us to become a teacher, one thing is inevitable: we have a certain degree of talent. The possession of talent is at once both fortunate and unfortunate, because what one person finds easy, others do not. For example we may have to struggle to learn how to play two quavers against a triplet at first but suddenly our minds grasp it and, like learning to ride a bicycle, we do not forget – it comes naturally. For others, it may never 'click'. This creates a barrier when it comes to teaching which, for some, is hard to break down. Occasionally, one hears a teacher say 'But it's easy!' Easy for them, yes, but for the child everything is difficult until he can do it.

The trouble with a dyslexic is that one day he may be able to conquer a particular problem and the next he may not. This is where patience comes in: patience in the teacher and also patience in the pupil. I think we sometimes forget that, if a pupil appears to have grasped some point and then comes along the next week without having capitalized on his new knowledge and apparently having forgotten all about it, it is in fact worse for him than it is for us. *We* are challenged to find a more colourful way of making that point more memorable and more relevant to his way of working. *He* has only demonstrated his forgetfulness again.

Most people know inside themselves that if they have a degree of talent, and with the help of an encouraging and understanding teacher who also believes in them, they can achieve in their chosen field. The relationship between teacher and pupil is necessarily a close one, and we all know that unless it is harmonious the pupil will not progress in the way he should. Technically, lack of self-esteem and confidence are normally recognized as secondary symptoms of dyslexia, but sometimes – and I suggest that when a child undertakes to have music lessons this can be one of the times – it is more important to treat the secondary symptoms before the primary symptoms. Secondary symptoms can have an effect on IQ scores and reading skills, so our efforts are a valuable contribution that we can make to the general welfare of our pupil. Every little success, even if it is the same one that was achieved the week before, has to be duly rewarded with praise – honest praise – so that his self-esteem is seen to grow steadily lesson by lesson. The child may have come to us with the feeling that he is making a fresh start outside the classroom: we can make or break his confidence with a word.

Anxiety caused by fear of the teacher will set up inhibitions in any pupil, and if that pupil is dyslexic, the inhibitions will be more like paralysis. Once or twice in my early teaching career, I have learnt to my horror that a child has been afraid of me. Perhaps I have been too fierce in my admonitions about practising, or perhaps I have leapt too quickly to correct mistakes, but one of the unavoidable truths about teaching children is that they can at times be very easily upset. Probably all of us can remember times when, as children, we were very upset by remarks that our elders and betters have made. We may have burned with indignation and gone to hide our tears in a corner somewhere. There is no escape for a child alone with a music teacher. Sometimes something in the child's environment – a sudden surprise, a sharp word or even the sheer size of the teacher casting a shadow over the keyboard – can temporarily unnerve him. Unless one is careful the rest of the lesson will be a waste of time.

Until one gets into the habit of it, it is quite hard for some of us constantly to bear in mind that the child's view of the world is not the same as the adult's. To take a simple example: if you have ever been back to some building you knew well as a child, you will probably have been amazed at how small it seemed when you returned. The proportions will have seemed quite different. When a child, you were impressed by the huge front door and how high you had to reach to ring the bell. As an adult, the door may have seemed quite ordinary, perhaps even rather small for the general façade, and you may have noticed that the bell was quite out of character with the other door furnishings. So it is with the proportional properties of events. It may be much more important to the proud owner of a new pair of shoes that the teacher notices them than that he plays his scales well.

If we are to be good teachers of dyslexics, we have to be in total accord, as far as is humanly possible, with our pupils. Their concerns have to be our concerns, their problems our problems and we will perhaps ultimately be allowed a share in their achievements. We have to forget the trophies on the mantelpiece and the lists of examination successes published in the local newspaper; if we teach a dyslexic, it may be a triumph much more rewarding if he eventually learns to give a reasonable rendering of a simple Grade 1 standard piece. An achievement is anything that he has learned to do which he originally found impossible, and it is by building up these little achievements that one gradually helps to build up that self-esteem that is so vital to his development.

Over the years, teachers will gradually work out methods of teaching specific points, for example the stave, basic rhythmic patterns, recognition of intervals or chord shapes, and so on, that they find easy to explain and seem to work best for their pupils. They also like to measure their pupils' progress by entering them occasionally for an examination, particularly in England but also anywhere in the world where the Associated Board of the Royal Schools of Music (ABRSM), or any other examining board, sends examiners. By no means all children or all teachers make use of what others see as a useful ladder of achievement, but it is a well-tried system and for many it works. All-round competence is tested, and if he passes, the student receives a certificate. Many teachers, even if they do not enter their pupils for examinations, tend to use this idea of all-round competence as a guide to what they teach.

When it comes to teaching a pupil with dyslexia, I suggest to you that we abandon this concept of teaching altogether and concentrate on how our pupil wants to learn. For example, it is not pleasant or helpful to him to insist on teaching him to understand the stave if he is susceptible to stressful visual stimuli such as a pattern of stripes (Wilkins et al., 1986). There are ways of presenting the stave differently (see Chapter 4), and eventually the child will probably want to learn about it. Then is the time to explain it. Similarly, he may find it impossible to keep his eyes on the music in front of him and simultaneously think about which of his fingers he is using. For him, it will be a real trial to practise trying to do this for a minute at a time, let alone 5 or 10 minutes every day for a week on his own. It would be much better to treat understanding the stave as a separate exercise altogether, and to teach him to play music without recourse to the written page. One day, he may want to try to conquer the problem, perhaps being motivated by wanting to learn new pieces faster or even by wanting to try taking an examination; meanwhile, he can learn so much about making music in other ways.

Many of our cherished ideas about how and when to teach specific points have to be discarded in favour of allowing the pupil, albeit unconsciously, to lead the way. One has to be intensely aware of what the dyslexic pupil is feeling and thinking. He must feel that he can challenge his teacher to explain something better, to find a more satisfying method of solving a difficulty or even to produce a more tuneful/exciting/colourful book. The pupil must feel free to say at once if he is confused, and he must be aware that the teacher knows that it is up to her to find a way. If that way is not found, the fault lies with her and not with him. One simply has to trust one's dyslexic pupil, and one has to convey that trust to him. This means that every lesson, although carefully planned, is an exploration together. It is a real challenge both to one's adaptability as a teacher and to one's imagination, but it can be immensely rewarding and stimulating. If we are really alive to the problems by identifying, as closely as we can, with our dyslexic pupils, we learn as much from them as they learn from us. This inevitably spills over into all our teaching. It is fun, it stimulates the imagination in all sorts of ways and one feels oneself grow as a teacher, as well as having the immense privilege of sharing in the rewards that, for our pupils, are so exciting and important.

Summary

The dyslexic child may have an equal right to learn the language of music, but it is extremely likely that he will not feel equal. He will have accumulated a very long list of experiences, particularly in the school environment, that will have persuaded him that life is loaded against him. More obvious disabilities, such as blindness or deafness, are understood, but the dyslexic child suffers from lack of understanding and, after a few years at school, his self-esteem may well be non-existent.

There are children who escape diagnosis as dyslexics for many years, but there are characteristics that should be recognizable by the instrumental music teacher. In fact, the instrumental music teacher, who has a one-to-one relationship with the pupil, is in a unique position to spot these characteristics. Much time and heartache – on both the part of the pupil and the teacher – can be saved if the teacher is alive to the possibility that the child might be dyslexic and what this will entail in any teaching programme.

The qualities of a teacher are paramount: *humility, adaptability, imagination, awareness* and *genuine interest* in the dyslexic child as a person are the ones I would venture to put first. *Humility*, in the acknowledgement that there will be difficulties to be overcome, which, through lucky chance, one has never had oneself and that one is in a privileged position to help our pupil to master. *Adaptability*, in that we will probably have to discard well-tried methods and concepts of the teacher as the leader in favour of encouraging the child himself to find the best way for him. *Imagination*, because without it one cannot do all these things and when imagination is rampant then patience becomes obsolete. *Awareness*, because the bond between pupil and teacher will only be forged if the pupil has confidence that the teacher is sensitive to all his problems and difficulties. This applies also to a *genuine interest* in the person one is teaching, and whether teacher and pupil together achieve great things or not, one can make the pupil feel that he is a person who matters and one can give him a sense of identity that he probably badly needs.

Chapter 3
Auditory problems

Specific training in aural awareness for the general musician is to a large extent a phenomenon of the twentieth century. Until the middle of the nineteenth century, it would seem that it was not considered necessary for the instrumentalist to have any particular ear training to assist him in his performance. Singers were the exception to the rule, but, in all the other branches of the art, specific training took second place to virtuosity and practical skill with the fingers. During the latter half of the nineteenth century, a new movement in music education evolved, led and encouraged by John Curwen in England and Émil Jaques-Dalcroze in France (see p. 10). They made aural perception the foundation of their methods, nurturing the musical roots of the individual well before the introduction of any serious instrumental instruction.

These two different approaches – the original, purely instrumental method and the method that began with aural perception – continued to develop side by side but did not mix. It was only in the early twentieth century that ear training was established as part of the curriculum in music conservatoires. It became acknowledged to be essential in the training of all musicians, and nowadays nearly every accepted music examination reflects this.

There is a school of thought that is of the opinion that all necessary aural training can be done within the context of the repertoire that the child is learning. There is a strong case for this, and the comparatively recent changes in the syllabus for the ABRSM aural tests reflect this attitude. Ear training is now seen as an integral constituent of repertoire. There are musical educators who have been advocating this for many years, and I am sure that it is here to stay.

Dyslexia manifests itself in many recognizable ways. Foremost among the problems that may occur is a difficulty with the sounds of language. The popularly held misconception that dyslexia, or Specific Learning Difficulty, is purely a visual problem is now widely recognized as only part of the truth. More and more people are beginning to realize that some of their apparently inexplicable problems may arise from some form of specific learning difficulty that is not directly related to their eyes. It may be that some children have an auditory problem at the root of or compounding their difficulties.

In this chapter, we consider some of the possible anomalies that may occur in auditory function or perception, and how they may be recognized. We also consider the confusions to which they may give rise and how we may go some of the way towards helping to dispel them.

Music teachers are naturally more interested in teaching music than in teaching children to read and write language, but the sharpening up of their aural ability in the field of music may well be of value when it comes to aural perception in language reading and, particularly, spelling. We examine here not only the problems that a dyslexic may have, both physically and conceptually, but also how to help him make better sense of what he hears.

Anomalies in auditory function

Although academic opinion is divided, it is a clear possibility that those children who are failing at reading and spelling have some weaknesses in auditory processing. We music teachers are sometimes faced with the problem of teaching children classed as dyslexics who come into this category. Ours is not to reason why – our job is to teach – but it does help to know what it is realistic to expect from one's pupils.

A quick, but not infallible, test to find out whether the pupil has a weakness in this area is to ask him whether he can repeat the words 'statistical' or 'preliminary'. It does not matter if the child has not heard these words before or if he is unaware of their meaning. What you are testing is whether he can accurately pick up and hold briefly in his memory a combination of short adjacent syllables. If he cannot you have learnt one of two things: either (1) that he has some weakness in auditory processing, or (2) that he cannot, for some reason, connected probably with a muscular problem, get his tongue round the words. It is too difficult for the layman to decide which of the two is the more likely to be correct, and for practical purposes it may not even be necessary. The importance of the information lies in an increased awareness of the problems that the child may have.

If you have used some multisyllabled words such as 'statistical' or 'preliminary' to test for auditory weaknesses, and have said the words reasonably slowly and distinctly, the problem may be one of short-term memory. The child may have no difficulty with pitch-based sounds and yet have difficulty with remembering speech-based sounds. He may not be able to remember the first syllable by the time you have reached the last one. Closely related may be his short-term memory for musical rhythm. Here is a problem that will have to be addressed carefully (see p. 38).

Some children who pass the normal hearing test administered by health authorities at the request of schools in the United Kingdom may nevertheless be subject to some form of *hearing loss*. The way to find out whether this is the case is to play a simple sound on the keyboard and ask him to listen to it with his eyes closed and to indicate in some way – perhaps by lifting his hand – when he can hear it no longer. This should be done choosing sounds of widely differing pitch.

He may have perfectly normal hearing from C below the bass stave to D above the treble stave, but above or below those sounds, his hearing may be either distorted or actually prone to some loss. Remember to test each ear individually by blocking the sound to the other ear, and to insist that he has his eyes closed. The conclusions you draw should be recorded – they may well be useful later on.

A knowledge of one's pupil's hearing capability is not only essential before one can formulate aural expectations for him, but is also helpful when it comes to deciding on which side of him one should sit when teaching. Other instrumentalists can move around – they can even stand or sit opposite their pupils – but pianists are usually confined to standing or sitting beside their pupils. The dyslexic child with a strong left ear and a weak right ear will naturally react more quickly and confidently to pitched sounds presented to his left ear, and it may be more comfortable for him if his teacher sits on his left.

If it is clear that the pupil has some form of auditory malfunction, what should we do? First, of course, the parents should be involved and the whole matter discussed fully, preferably with the cooperation of the school. Much useful information that may affect the child can be pooled and acted upon positively.

Second, in order to get the results that the music demands and which are normally achieved by being controlled by the ear, it may be advisable to recognize that this approach is unlikely to be successful on its own, so it may be better to concentrate on the physical side of what is required.

Here is a simple example (Figure 3.1). This little Mozart Arioso demands a feminine ending to the first phrase, but in order to be in position for the following phrase, it is necessary to play the F in bar 2 with the 2nd finger. This means that the G has to be played with a strong third finger, and many children, unless they have been taught to listen, will land on it with a comfortable thump and will probably start feeling for the D without listening for the quaver rest at all. Indeed, there is a lot to listen for here that the dyslexic may not be capable of doing. Far better then to concentrate on the feel of a dropped wrist on the F followed by a wrist-led float off the G and get the *action* right. The quiet G and the rest will both be accomplished – and all that remains will be to try to get the child to play the quaver D softly.

Mozart: Arioso

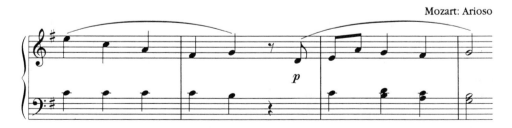

Figure 3.1.

Auditory laterality

One occasionally hears the term 'cross-lateral'. A person is considered to be cross-lateral when hand and eye are oppositely lateralized, for example right-handed and left-eyed. (Thomson, 1990). As with our hands and eyes, most people have a dominant ear. Sounds of all descriptions are heard by both ears and are mostly sent to the opposite side of the brain to be processed. In the latter half of the twentieth century, it has become widely, but not universally, accepted that whereas the left side of the brain is specialized for language, analytical and logical processing and musical rhythm, the right side of the brain is specialized for musical pitch and tonality, spatial perception and form perception (Borchgrevink, 1982) (see Chapter 1). Assuming that this is correct, the analysis of a musical phrase will therefore require both sides of the brain to work with perfect coordination: the left side to process the rhythm, and the right side to process the pitch and tonality. If a dyslexic has a strongly dominant left ear, it is likely that he will be much better at understanding pitch than at understanding rhythm, the reverse being the case if he has a strongly dominant right ear.

The simplest way to discover which is the dominant ear is to put a watch with a decent tick down on the table or the piano lid, and ask the child to put his ear close to the watch, until he can hear it ticking. He will automatically present his dominant ear to the watch, but, to make sure, ask him to do it again. It is better to vary the task the second time, so if you have a small transistor radio handy, turn the volume down extremely low and ask him whether he can hear what is being broadcast. Place the radio or watch immediately in front of him. If he presents the other ear the second time, you will know that his ears have mixed laterality, which means that neither one is dominant. If this is the case, his reactions to pitch and rhythm will probably vary, but if he always presents the same ear it is clear which of the two musical elements will need the most training.

The majority of my dyslexic pupils have shown a marked left-ear dominance. This means that the sounds that they hear mainly travel more strongly to the right hemisphere of the brain – the hemisphere which is normally best for performing the task of processing musical sounds. This is good for general musical appreciation, but not so good for disentangling rhythm or for language-based skills, which are normally processed in the left hemisphere.

There are sometimes dyslexics who show no particular dominance. There is some evidence to suggest that these children hear sounds more strongly in the ear that best accepts the frequency of that particular sound. This has particular relevance to how children hear and analyse the extremely diverse sounds of speech and may be an extra difficulty for someone with dyslexic tendencies. However, if we ascertain which ear is dominant in our dyslexic pupil, we know better what to expect, and we can work out strategies to overcome problems that may arise.

If the child has left ear dominance, the *first* strategy in rhythm exercises is to try to get him to listen with his right ear. This can be done by asking him to close his left ear with the index finger of his left hand. This tactic immediately dulls the left ear and stimulates the right ear. It will feel unfamiliar to him and he may not enjoy doing it, but if the reason for doing it is explained to him, he will probably enter into the experiment with greater enthusiasm.

The *second* strategy is to separate the rhythm from the pitch and work on each separately, remembering that the rhythmic aspect is going to need much more attention than the pitch.

If the pupil has right ear dominance, it is possible that rhythm *per se* will not be a difficulty, but he may have difficulty with organizing his response to pitch. He may also have a problem fitting rhythm and pitch together. Again, they should be worked at separately and broken down into very simple components.

Silence – the framework for music

We all recognize now that aural training in its broadest sense is crucial to the understanding and appreciation of music of all kinds. We also know that unless a child has learnt to listen to himself, not just playing the notes but also giving expression to the music within them, the result will be unsatisfactory for the child and painful for his audience.

That is not to say that the child with no formal aural training will not enjoy music – his fancy may well be tickled by catchy tunes or powerful rhythms – but if anything deeper is to be achieved, he is likely to need help. For the sake of his own performance, he will need to learn to listen acutely, simply so that he can distinguish right from wrong. This will in turn rub off on his appreciation of other performances besides his own and may lead to the more abstract consideration of what the music is trying to convey.

There are few teachers who are lucky enough to teach in an ideal situation: an adequately heated, peaceful room with plenty of space, free from tiresome interruption of any kind. Most of us have to put up with at least one disadvantage, and I suspect that the most common one is that of extraneous sound. This can be, should be and probably is readily turned to advantage by the listening teacher. There will be many who have asked their pupils to count up all the sounds that they can hear during a couple of minutes of 'silence' and stillness in the room. This is sometimes the first time that a child has really listened, and it can be most revealing both to the teacher and to the child. He may hear a dog bark or the sound of footsteps in the distance but completely miss the tick of a clock in the room or the drone of an aeroplane high in the sky.

Two whole minutes can be quite a long time for a dyslexic child to concentrate entirely on listening. If the pupil is easily distracted, it may be advisable to suggest only one minute. Besides being a small step towards more acute listening, this is a useful ploy to have up one's sleeve for the child who finds concentration difficult.

I always encourage pupils to close their eyes during the 'silence', and I make sure that they are sitting comfortably. If there are any visual distractions, they do not listen nearly as well, and if they have their eyes shut, they also become more aware of their own bodies, so that something like a nose that needs blowing or a sock that is slipping down assumes a disproportionate importance and can be an added distraction.

At times, I have introduced extra sounds into the 'silence' after about 30 seconds. A child may tune his ears to one or two obvious sounds in the distance and then be unable to retune them to a quiet tapping or swishing sound in the foreground. Once he becomes aware that he may be caught out by the deliberate intervention of a new sound, an element of excitement and heightened listening creeps into the game, and it becomes much more fun. Sometimes, one can exchange tasks with the pupil and give him the pleasure of trying to outwit his teacher. He will probably be devious in the extreme, but that does not matter; all that matters is that he becomes more aware of what listening really is, so that he can bring his best listening skills to every field in which they are needed.

In addition to listening training and its use as practice in concentration, suggesting that the pupil spends a minute listening also involves the short-term auditory memory. The silence must not be broken by speech; he has to remember the sounds he has heard so that he can recite them afterwards. It is a good idea to suggest that he counts them silently on his fingers so that at the end of the listening period he knows how many he has to remember. It is, in effect, an auditory adaption of the game known as Kim's game, in which the players are given a short space of time to memorize as many objects on a tray as possible and are then required to make a list of them.

We all will have come across children who begin to talk before the sound of their playing has died away, or even those who give a running commentary of their performance as they go along! Learning to listen to silence is good practice for starting and finishing a performance. It introduces a moment of calm, during which the player eventually learns to rehearse in his mind the sounds he is about to produce, or listens for the echo of the final chord. It also helps him to listen during performance to the sounds he is actually making.

Any child will benefit from learning to become more aware of sound. A dyslexic with a poor auditory memory needs more practice than most in concentrating on what he hears – in other words, on *listening* – and also on being able to recall what he has heard. If he performs the task well, the length of listening time can be increased next time and possibly recorded in his notebook (see p.122). In my experience, it is not a good idea to play this game every week – the novelty wears off – but it adds variety for a pupil who is easily distracted and can be beneficial in the several ways that I have outlined.

The concept of 'up' and 'down'

The dyslexic child may exhibit a confusion about terms when first beginning to learn to listen to music. One of the most frequent difficulties seems to be over the concept of 'up' and 'down'. It is hard for us non-dyslexics to grasp that such a concept should cause a problem, but it undoubtedly does, just as left and right all too often do. For the child, the sounds he hears may well be 'different' from one another but he may not have begun to order them into higher and lower. Tonal discrimination is needed for aural tests in examinations, so, when concentrating on pitch, one first has to make quite sure that the pupil relates the word 'up' with a higher sound and the word 'down' with a lower sound.

It is not enough to rely on mere words, even if one is demonstrating by playing high and low sounds and perhaps even waving one's hands in the air. A meaningful way of relating high sounds to the word 'high' and low sounds to the word 'low' must be found for him. This point is of continual importance. It may be necessary to discuss with him at length how he perceives sounds: he may not have the same understanding as we do of the terms we normally use. If the pupil has shown any tendency to be confused, he will need to experience the feeling of high and low within himself so that he internalizes the terms enough for them to become absolutely automatic.

One simple way to help him with this is to get him to sing slowly up the scale with accompaniment on the piano, moving his hand slowly up from the abdomen and arriving at the top of his head and the top of the scale at the same time. To accentuate the feeling of producing high sounds and low sounds with the voice, he should then sing the words 'Up High' at the top of the octave and 'Down Low' at the bottom.

The piano keyboard is basically flat, and horizontal to the floor, but the further to the right the keys are played, the higher the sound that is made. Similarly the further to the left, the lower the sound. Ben (see p.7) solved the problem when it came to reading notes on the page and translating them onto the keyboard by using stickers on the piano. He soon learnt that if the note was higher on the page, it would sound higher. What took longer was helping him to experience high and low away from both the page and the keyboard. Given only two sounds to distinguish, he could identify the higher or lower sound, but faced with a short tune, for example that in Figure 3.2, he would be unable to imagine the shape of it, and his conception of high and low seemed to desert him. He could not hold the earlier sounds in his head in order to compare them each with each .

Figure 3.2.

Ben needed to have the tune played to him several times very slowly, he needed to sing it, feeling each sound in his head and mouth, he needed to make the shape of it in the air as he sang, until finally he was able to draw an approximation of it on a blank piece of paper as in Figure 3.3. In other words the problem had to be tackled multisensorily.

Figure 3.3.

Sometimes it is difficult to judge whether a pupil has the same concept as we do. For example, he may be able to recite the alphabet backwards from G, but are the sounds he utters meaningful to him? Can he recite backwards from E without having to start from G again? Does he know which letters are on either side of C?

The musician will never be thoroughly conversant with reading music and understanding his instrument unless he can recognize instantaneously that, for example, E is situated between D and F. It is not enough for him to be able to work it out by starting from A every time. The pianist may have more difficulty with this than do other instrumentalists because all the white notes are adjacent to one another and look and feel the same. The string player develops a different concept of the orientation of notes because of their relation to the different strings on his instrument. Each different instrumentalist has his own concept of what notes mean to him, but when it comes to reading or writing music, they all need the same basic skills of recognition.

The dyslexic may need help by means of plastic letters, feeling each one and listening to the sound, before he feels comfortable with those seven letters. The letters can be placed in a circle so that no one letter takes precedence over another, and practice should be by reading both clockwise and anticlockwise, as well as in reading every alternate letter name, up to a maximum of three, in preparation for the triad.

Singing

The voice to which all children react best is their own. There are now techniques available to dyslexics learning to read and spell that exploit this idea, using recordings of their own voices. In the music lesson, a child can be encouraged to sing along with his playing, especially when learning scales and arpeggios. This introduces a new aid to learning that can complement the normal, narrower methods in a more personal and vibrant way.

Some children love singing; some are afraid to sing. For whatever reason they fear singing, it is important that they overcome their fear and, if possible, learn to love it. Dyslexics who can sing relatively well have another dimension to their music-making, which is of great value. It helps them to feel within themselves the shape of tunes; it encourages them to understand phrasing; it gives them a stronger sense of progression; it is good practice for the memory. The breath control necessary for singing is physically beneficial, and if they can sing well it is good for their self-confidence.

We have all met the 'droners': those children who believe that their voices are rising and falling to order but who are actually singing almost entirely on one note all the time. It used to be the custom to call these unfortunate children 'tone-deaf' and to write them off as being musically beyond hope. 'Tone-deaf' is still an expression that is bandied about, but there are now educators and thinkers (Wisbey, Froseth, etc.) who are doing much to overcome this attitude. I have always firmly believed that tone-deafness is a myth. 'Droners' are not necessarily dyslexic, but, for those who are, the following suggestions for remediation of this problem may be useful.

What seems to be the first requirement in the development of these children is an awareness of pitch and an ability to hear themselves.

There is a school of thought that suggests that one should first of all identify the sound which the child *can* sing and then gradually work on extending the range from that point. The advantage of this method is that the child begins with success. You say to him at the beginning of your aural work, which, if he is a droner, is at first best done separately from his playing, 'Can you sing this sound?', and you play, or sing, 'his' note. He pipes up with his only sound and you say, 'Yes, that's right'. Instant success, but now comes the difficult bit. If you play a tone higher or lower for him to imitate, he will stay put on 'his' note. You now start to employ other strategies to get him to vary the pitch. You can suggest that he hums, sings to 'oo' etc., and one day you may chance upon something that works, perhaps for no other reason than that he is now a little older, but while you are waiting for that to happen, you will have had to respond to his efforts a good many times with something like 'That was a good try. Now let's try another one', which avoids telling him he is wrong but does not give him the pleasure of knowing that he has been successful. It can turn into rather a sterile and dispiriting experience for both teacher and pupil. Nor does it help to foster that awareness of pitch that is so essential.

The method I now prefer is to approach the whole subject from the extremes of pitch and work inwards. One can ask the child to imitate some of the sounds he hears around him in everyday life: the squeak of a car braking, or the sound of a car engine being revved up, a fire siren or the sound of his – or your – doorbell. When he makes his imitations, which he will do without consciously thinking about pitch, he should be encouraged to put his hand on that part of his body where he can best feel the vibrations of the sound. If one asks him for a more 'musical' or midrange sound, he will probably look at one blankly and be unable to feel anything; the throat/mouth sounds are the hardest. On the other hand the 'brmm – brmm' of a revving engine will usually prompt a hand on his chest, whereas the squeal of an iron gate will prompt a hand on the top of his head. (Children have such wonderful imagination. One pupil – a former 'droner' – arrived one day with her hair plaited in a pigtail on the top of her head. When the time arrived for some aural work I said to her, 'Sing this sound through your pigtail' and she immediately produced a top E!) Any number of other sounds can be suggested, with as wide a variation in pitch as possible, until he becomes automatically aware of what resonating surfaces he uses to make imitations of these sounds. Sometimes it is helpful to suggest to him that he holds his nose, or blocks his ears, in order to hear himself more clearly. Eventually he learns to reproduce a siren, or a two-tone doorbell or something similar, using first the high head resonators and second the low chest resonators. He begins to learn that different sounds feel different, and his awareness of pitch is awakened. The muscles needed to control the pitch of the voice will need a great deal more practice, but the first steps away from the stationary note will have been made. Provided he is not asked to hum or sing anything too fast, and provided that it is only one or, at the most, two sounds at a time, he may, by being asked to think about where on his body those sounds will resonate, be able to give a fair approximation of them. The drone will have gone.

In addition to making steps towards solving the 'drones' problem, this method of working on sound reinforces from a new angle the concept of the high and low – which as we have seen, may be a difficulty for the dyslexic. He learns to feel internally, as well as externally, the difference between them.

Rhythm

Rhythm is the web that holds all music together; an understanding of rhythm therefore underpins the foundation of all our musical endeavours.

Much of what we loosely call rhythm is, in fact, the pulse beat underlying the music. The pulse beat is basic to all rhythmic variation, and it is often this which a dyslexic pupil finds difficult to maintain. If one asks him to clap a crotchet pulse beat while one plays simple crotchets, there is no difficulty, but if one then breaks into quavers, or indulges in an occasional minim, he finds it hard to keep steady. This is because he is not really feeling the pulse of the music throughout his body: clapping in time has become a cerebral occupation that can easily be upset when other cerebral considerations start to interfere. He needs to be encouraged to feel the beat internally.

It might be helpful here to draw attention to the fact that aural *discrimination* and the *ability to perform* in response to aural discrimination can be two entirely different skills. The child who can *hear* ♩ ♫ ♩ and can *distinguish* it from ♩ ♫ ♩ when it is performed by his teacher may not have the muscle control necessary to make a clear distinction between the two rhythms when he is asked to perform them on his own. Clumsiness being one of the characteristics to which dyslexics are prone, we have to be careful to ascertain that this is not a factor that we wrongly attribute to his aural ability alone.

Those who are familiar with Dalcroze eurythmics (see p.10) will no doubt use many of Jaques-Dalcroze's methods for ensuring that their pupils 'live' the music within themselves. Unfortunately, we do not all have the space to encourage our pupils to dance and run round the room. Sometimes there is only enough space to march on the spot! But one can improvise other methods. They may not be as good, but they are better than nothing, although for dyslexics who may have poor coordination, they have the advantage of simplicity. Dalcroze expects his pupils to be able to combine several activities, including catching balls. As a second best to Dalcroze, I suggest using a tape-recorder, as Froseth does for large classes of children (see p.11).

The method is simple. The teacher and the pupil sit opposite one another with plenty of freedom to move both arms and legs from a sitting position. The tape recorder is turned on and the teacher, having first chosen a good rhythmic piece of music, sets up a series of simple movements, in time to the music, which the pupil copies. The teacher may begin by clapping or stamping or some similar, very simple, exercise. The pupil copies, acting as a mirror image. When the pupil has happily settled in to the exercise, that exercise is changed by the teacher, without breaking the continuity of the idea of movement. The initial movements should always be big and bold. Gradually all the limbs are involved – at first one at a time, but later, as the pupil gets more experienced and quicker at picking up the lead set by the teacher, movements can be combined to include two, three and possibly even more limbs according to the imagination of the teacher and the ability of the pupil.

Having thoroughly loosened up and involved the whole body in feeling the pulse beat, I always allow my pupils to change roles with me and make me copy them. They love doing this, and even the shyest pupil invariably ends up laughing. It is also revealing: a dyslexic pupil finds it very hard to think up a new activity while continuing with the old one. At first, he will have to stop and start again or be at risk of losing touch with the beat. I usually suggest to my pupils who are most at risk of breaking the continuity that, if they need to stop in order to think up a new exercise, I will give them a count of 8, or possibly 6, before they must start again. When they do stop, I whisper the count quietly.

This exercise is a useful preliminary to the ABRSM aural tests in Grades 1–3. It can be expanded to include setting up a rhythmic response: the pupil *imagining* himself to be copying the teacher for a couple of bars and then actually joining in for two bars before stopping to watch and *imagine* for two more bars, etc. It is more of a whole body experience and is the basis for the simple test of ability, which is what the ABRSM sets out to examine.

Preparation for aural examinations

The non-dyslexic child usually has sufficient impetus and sense of direction for the teacher to be able to integrate the training for aural examinations into the work he is doing on his pieces. He can switch easily from thinking about fingering, which is a motor number exercise, to thinking about intervals, which is an auditory number exercise, but which has a totally different slant to it. He can then return to thinking about fingering without feeling disturbed, often in fact having benefited from a temporary change of direction.

Not so the dyslexic. Dyslexics spend so much of their time drifting in a world that other people seem to understand but they do not. Many of them are forced along by the current of human existence, knowing that they are not in charge. They need to know where they stand. They need to know what the lesson is about and they need time to readjust from one subject to the next.

The whole subject of aural training is therefore much better approached as if it were unconnected with learning to play a piece of music, even if one is longing to say 'Listen! Have you noticed that the interval at the beginning of the tune this time is a 5th instead of a 4th?' It would only throw him off balance and muddle him. He must be allowed to concentrate on only one thing at a time.

If there is any doubt about what he is being asked to do, he should be encouraged to explain what he thinks has been asked of him. Sometimes, the question itself needs to be discussed in his terms before any attempt is made at answering it.

As there are several questions in aural examinations that depend upon having a good auditory memory, which is where a dyslexic may have a deficit, it can be helpful to suggest to him that he indicates in some way the moment he hears what it is that he is supposed to be listening for. If he waits until one has finished playing, he may be unable to explain what he has heard, even though he may have noticed the relevant point at the time when he heard it. If he is allowed to interrupt at the crucial moment, his confidence in his ability is strengthened.

One of the most important considerations when training or testing the ear is that of speed. If the child has any delay in auditory processing, it should go without saying that allowances should be made for this. Tunes for singing or rhythms for clapping should be short enough for the child to remember and slow enough for him to be able to hear clearly. It is far better to start with something easy, even if it is well short of the objective.

One needs to consider not only the speed at which one presents musical sounds to the pupil but also – and I believe that this is often overlooked – the speed of one's own voice when giving instructions or asking questions. It is important to say what one has to say as simply as possible and to speak at a speed that is comfortable for the pupil. The dyslexic tires more easily than the non-dyslexic, and if the speed of one's speech is too quick for him, he will inevitably 'switch off'.

It will be obvious to any teacher that, unless a pupil has heard a tune correctly, he will not be able to reproduce it. In order to check that he is hearing it correctly, it is sometimes helpful to ask him to move his hand up and down in the air to give an approximation of the distances between the sounds of the tune. This can be done as the teacher plays the tune for the second time. He may prefer to draw the rise and fall of the tune on a piece of paper. Either way, this is another application of the multisensory approach to teaching, as well as being a useful check that the pupil is aware of what he is hearing.

The memorizing of rhythmic patterns is often assisted by marching around the room. Sometimes, it is possible to allow the pupil to start marching before one begins to play the rhythm one wishes him to memorize. He will choose a pace comfortable for himself. One then picks up the beat for the basis of the rhythm. This means that, having set the beat going within himself, all he now has to do is to superimpose the rhythm. In other words there is one less problem with which he has to cope.

The huge range of the piano is an asset sometimes not fully exploited by teachers. When one is helping a dyslexic pupil to learn a musical phrase – whether it be for aural or practical purposes – it will take many times the 'normal' number of repetitions to fix it in his memory. There are seven and a half octaves on the piano keyboard, so use can be made of all of them. Tunes should be transposed at the octave. Not only will this ensure that the passage is practised many times over, but the ear will also benefit from the alteration in pitch. (A limited adaptation of this idea can be used by the string player but not, of course, by those playing wind instruments.) A change is as good as a rest! – and children often love to hear their tunes sounding unusually rich and sonorous in the bass or light and tinkling at the top of the keyboard.

We all react to some sounds more favourably than to others. For example, some children instinctively know which instrument they wish to learn to play the moment they hear it. Occasionally, the quality of the sound seems to provoke a musical reaction and an affinity with the instrument that is quite uncanny. If we can discover the sort of sound that our dyslexic pupil reacts to best, we – and he – are much more likely to succeed. Many a teacher will have extracted the correct reply from her pupil to an aural test by singing it to him instead of playing it on the piano, or by tapping on the piano lid – which produces a richer resonance – instead of simply clapping.

A dyslexic whose hearing is impaired for certain frequencies might find that he could produce a better response to an aural test if that test were administered at a different pitch. Eventually, of course, he must learn to cope with sounds on any frequency, but, in the early stages, changing the pitch can be helpful.

Summary

It would be wrong to assume that, because a child has been labelled dyslexic, he is therefore going to have a problem with aural training. This aspect of learning about music is often a dyslexic's strength and, as such, can be developed and exploited in all the well-recognized ways, giving him ample opportunity to enjoy success.

There may, however, be some children who suffer from some developmental delay or possibly a minor degree of distortion or loss of hearing that is not instantly apparent to the casual observer. Before beginning any formal aural work, it would be helpful to investigate to what extent your dyslexic pupil is hearing in the normal way and to ascertain which is his dominant ear. This may be a factor in his dyslexic tendencies, and it could also be apparent in his musical development. It is helpful to all concerned with the welfare of the child to discuss anything that has been discovered in the course of a music lesson with the parents. It is also advisable to recognize the limits within which realistic goals can be set.

Any confusion that a pupil may have over basic terms should be dispelled. Once this is done in all aural activities, be they rhythmic, melodic or merely learning to listen in silence, the speed – the elapse of time involved – will be a crucial factor. A dyslexic does not react well to being pressurized. Several factors that to us may appear trivial can have an adverse effect; even the speed of the teacher's voice may be one of these.

Pitch has an important part to play. The huge range of the keyboard offers ample opportunity for repetition to reinforce motor function, memory training and both rhythmic and melodic discrimination. Extremes of pitch can also be a springboard to enable the less-gifted singer to begin to understand his voice better.

All aural activities, be they melodic or rhythmic, are more liable to succeed if they can be approached as a whole 'body experience'. Singing can be used to encourage this. Reacting rhythmically to recorded music with the teacher also adds a fun element that challenges without stress. In fact, the aural aspect of learning to play an instrument, which is inextricably linked with all other aspects but which should be considered an activity on its own for dyslexics, is often the most pleasurable and satisfying part of the lesson for both the pupil and the teacher.

Chapter 4
Visual problems

The most widely accepted understanding of dyslexia among the general public is that dyslexics 'see letters back to front'. There are two assumptions here: (1) that there is a visual problem, and (2) that this results in a mirror image. For some dyslexics, in some instances, this may be true, but it is by no means an accurate or complete picture. In this chapter, this understanding is expanded and I show how the vagaries to which the eye/brain relationship is prone can appear to affect, or be affected by, the symbols we use for music.

There will be some advice on how some of the problems encountered can be circumvented. We all pick up useful tips from other teachers all the time and match them to our pupils' needs. In most cases, the following suggestions have been triggered by my pupils, but as every student's problems are different, other teachers may find that the suggestions have to be adapted.

Interpreting the printed page

Before music was written down, the emphasis was entirely on what was heard. As tunes were passed from generation to generation, there will inevitably have been modifications, elaborations or simplifications, but ever since the introduction of written music, there has been an increasingly slavish, on balance commendable, adherence to the written page. Even cadenzas have been notated and copied note for note. In the latter half of the twentieth century, a certain amount of freedom has crept in again, I am glad to say, but we still, thanks to painstaking musicologists, do our best to be loyal to what the great (and not so great) composers actually wrote. This necessitates very careful interpretation of the page in front of us. There is such a wealth of music, with more being written and published every day, that the emphasis has shifted from the ear to the eye in the learning of new work. It has become obligatory to give one's pupils books of music: they expect it, and some would feel deprived if one did not do it. There are strong arguments for not giving dyslexic pupils any form of commercially produced *primer*, because even the simplest of these has a wealth of written language material in it, and this is where the dyslexic is already failing. However, it is only realistic to recognize that the pupil will eventually want to buy a book of pieces. So even if pupils have problems with visual perception, they need to understand what is in front of them.

There is a very important consideration here. When we read keyboard music, for example, we are translating what we see on a flat vertical surface at eye level into what we do with our fingers on a stepped horizontal surface several inches below eye level. The visual adjustment that has to be made is difficult, sometimes very difficult, for a dyslexic pupil. This, in my experience, is an overriding problem, and the only answer that I can advocate is the avoidance of the necessity to make any adjustment. This means that if he is reading from the music, then he must do exactly that, and never take his eyes off it. A quick flick of the eyes down to the keyboard to make sure that the next interval is correctly judged is just not an option for him; he will lose his place and become thoroughly disorientated. He cannot concentrate on two visual planes at once.

There is another consideration where reading the score is concerned, which, for the dyslexic pianist, has considerable significance. The treble stave is situated above the bass stave on the page but on the keyboard the hand that plays the notes on the treble stave is on the right. Therefore the player has to feel comfortable with the idea that high means right and low means left. This involves two basic concepts with which the dyslexic may already be having difficulty: the concept of high and low, and the concept of left and right.

That the conflict between these concepts exists has been recognized since the early years of the twentieth century. There have been attempts to reconcile the way in which music is printed with the way in which some people prefer to think. The most notable attempt is perhaps that which resulted in the Klavarscribo method of printing music, which was invented in Holland and Russia simultaneously and is still in worldwide use today. The page is read from top to bottom in columns, as one would read a newspaper, the notes for the left hand being printed on the left of the column and the notes for the right hand on the right. The treble and bass staves are not used, but the lines that constitute the column bear direct relationship to the black notes on the keyboard. This method is well worth investigation (see 'Useful addresses').

A similar reconciliation of left and right with low and high can be created if one turns a page of music on its side. The treble stave is then on the right of the bass stave. The picture can be enhanced by writing all stems of treble clef notes upwards, which will become to the right, and bass clef stems downwards to the left. Some music written in this way is now marketed (see 'Useful addresses'). I have no personal experience of teaching a dyslexic pupil consistently to read music in this way, but I now use the trick of turning the page temporarily on its side when there is any question of the pupil being unable to relate the score to the keyboard.

At the outset, it must be understood that, in this chapter, 'reading music' merely applies to interpreting the traditional printed page as a preliminary or as an adjunct to learning the music in depth. Although the implications of what has been written down apply equally well to the performance of the music, whether it is being read at sight or after many hours of careful perusal, the art of 'sight-reading' comes into a different category and will be considered at a later stage. First of all we must ensure that deciphering the musical code is made as easy as possible for our pupil.

At every stage of this process, it is important to involve *the child* in all the decisions that are taken. It is often much quicker and tidier if the teacher plies an eradicator or a highlighter, etc, but it should ultimately be the pupil's decision how and when they are used. If he is particularly keen to do it himself, he should not be prevented, but I usually find that pupils are more interested in making music than in reading or writing it, and they are often not very confident about their fine motor skills.

Useful tools

For the purpose of editing the score, here is a list of useful tools to have handy:

*   several large photocopies of the music to be studied;
*   typist's white ink eradicator – 'Tipp-Ex' or equivalent;
*   white self-stick labels;
*   coloured highlighters;
*   black and red pens;
*   ruler, rubber and pencils.

Other teaching aids could include:

*   coloured 'post-it' labels;
*   a small adjustable frame (see p. 47);
*   coloured acetate;
*   clear plastic sleeves;
*   overhead projector pen;
*   plenty of plain paper;
*   jumbo-sized manuscript paper.

With this array of equipment, one is ready at any time to cover troublesome passages and 'personalize' them with something more helpful.

After all, what one is aiming for is the enjoyment of music. How one arrives at the faithful interpretation of what the composer intended is a matter for the performer. The route that has been followed to arrive at the desired result does not particularly matter provided that nobody else has to follow it in the same way. The listener does not need to know what weird devices and stratagems have been employed. The sound is what matters. There are accepted paths and conventions, but the text *per se* is not sacrosanct. As long as the sound is not violated, the score can be treated to all sorts of drastic editing[1], as it frequently is even by a non-dyslexic. When he is familiar with the music on the page and has internalized the sound, the child may well want to play his piece from memory, especially if his strengths are aural and tactile. That is fine, but first things first. Let us examine what written music consists of and how it may appear to a dyslexic.

---

[1]One important point should be made here, which is that several photocopies of pieces may be needed but that it is, as all should know, illegal under the laws of copyright to use a photocopy for anything other than specific teaching purposes.

The stave

Learning to play a musical instrument and to read music challenges every aspect of difficulty that a dyslexic encounters, none perhaps more so than the difficulty he may have in interpreting what his eyes perceive. The music student has to read a multitude of symbols written, not along one line in strict succession as in a book, but along a five-line stave and dotted about all over the place. Keyboard players have to contend with two staves (three for an organist), with many other complications, such as the pedals or indications to play an octave higher or lower. If he reads from the music, his eyes have to maintain a horizontal progression from left to right while constantly referring to the vertical.

The advantage that music has over the written word is that the pitch of each note is invariable and its duration is also proportionately invariable. If a reader of words encounters an A, he has to decide whether it is an a as in 'hat', a as in 'calm', a as in 'hate', a as in 'watch', or even whether he has to sound it at all, as in 'please'. As far as the pianist is concerned, he does not have to conjure up the sound in his own head before he plays it. It is a help if he can, and with practice he may be able to, but it is not a *sine qua non* for making music. This can make the piano, for a student with poor visual/motor coordination and possibly unreliable pitch, a helpful instrument to learn in spite of what may seem at times its daunting complexity. A above middle C is fixed at 440 cycles per second whatever instrument is played. On the piano, it is always found in exactly the same place, whereas there are several ways of finding the same sound on a stringed instrument, although all rely on the ear for complete precision of pitch. The ear has to guide the lips of wind players too, thus crowding the brain with an added responsibility. With a keyboard instrument, each named sound has its own particular visible place. For example, the pianist can see the place for an A sound. Once a student has learnt how to find the note on the piano shown in Figure 4.1, he is secure in the knowledge that it will always be in the same place and will sound at the same pitch. This stability instantly inspires confidence in the beginner – he can see as well as hear that he has got it right.

Figure 4.1

The symbol for the duration of any sound is harder to assimilate, but within the beat a minim will always be half the duration of a semibreve, a crotchet half the duration of a minim and so on. This is, of course, the same for any instrument. There are problems of interpretation when it comes to incorporating an accelerando or rallentando, but the principle remains the same.

Stave notation has been the subject of nearly a millenium of experiment and development, ever since Guido d'Arezzo's set of visually equidistant parallel lines in the eleventh century. It is interesting to note that d'Arezzo used different coloured lines to denote the absolute pitch (yellow for C, red for F). The same idea is still used today with modifications (C is red and F is black) for the strings of the harp. This is a useful visual aid that might well be worth employing for dyslexics. Colour was also used for many years by some practitioners to denote the duration of a sound. It was not until the early fifteenth century that scribes began to use hollow black notes for longer sounds. From the second quarter of the fifteenth century onwards, the stave for ensemble music became standardized at five lines, although in Italy and England more than five lines continued to be used right into the seventeenth century. Colouration was used less and less. It is creeping back again, notably in some recorder music for beginners in which every note has a colour attached, but the vast mass of music that we use today is printed black on white.

For a dyslexic, the problems start with the stave itself. Until recently, there was a theory of vision, basically accurate, which suggested that the optic nerve conveyed to one area of the brain what the eye saw and that this was interpreted by a different area. Further discoveries have now been made which suggest that there are several parallel streams of visual information passing through the brain, one of which is concerned with the analysis of movement. This can be activated not just by movement itself but by the illusion of movement, such as is induced by various types of modern art that make use of parallel lines and circles. It will probably be many years before the answers to the intriguing questions that these new discoveries pose will be answered, but, if areas of the brain are activated by the illusion of movement that parallel lines can create, there must be some significance for the dyslexic musician. It has been suggested (Wilkins et al., 1984) that anomalous visual effects can be caused by printed text forming a pattern of stripes, which can cause discomfort to those who are susceptible to such things. There is no doubt that parallel lines of text in a book can give rise to an impression of movement for some students with specific learning difficulties.

The very first tool of the music composer's trade consists of five parallel lines. Introducing the complete five-line stave, with its accompanying stave bracketed above or below it, is not necessarily, from my observation, a helpful way to start for some dyslexics. They are immediately challenged by a visual phenomenon that can upset them. Tunes abound in many beginners' books that use the notes shown in Figure 4.2.

Figure 4.2

These tunes incorporate the leger line for middle C, adding to the proliferation of lines. In order to learn the principle of tonal differentiation using lines and spaces it is a good idea to start with one line only, drawn across a blank sheet of paper. The same tunes can be written out using the C line only (Figure 4.3a), with the right hand (RH) highlighted in red or a colour of the pupil's choice.

Figure 4.3a

When the pupil has learnt to play this, he can progress to Figure 4.3b and then to Figure 4.3c, in which the continuity of the line is broken.

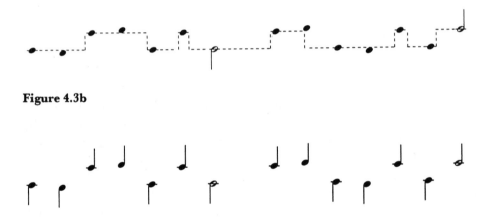

Figure 4.3b

Figure 4.3c
© 1967, 1981 by Faber Music Ltd, 3 Queen Square, London WC1N 3AU. Reproduced from *Piano Lessons Book 1* with kind permission of the publishers

Finally, he may move on to the printed copy, where the rests, dynamic markings and bar lines will be encountered and can be explained. The title of this piece 'Left! Right!', by Waterman/Harewood. is apposite and helpful for dyslexics who have any left/right confusion.

It is understandable but unfortunate, particularly for dyslexics, that beginners' books for pianists almost invariably start with pieces centred around middle C, necessitating the introduction of a leger line, whichever hand plays it. Many children do not appreciate that it *is* a leger line – they tend to think that it is just a special-looking note that is used for middle C. They also occasionally think that any note with a short line through it must be middle C, wherever it is orientated.

Whether the child is dyslexic or not, middle C has to be clearly demonstrated as the meeting place in the middle where the treble and bass clefs converge.

One continuous line for middle C, as in Figure 4.3a, helps to consolidate the principle that the two staves, although some distance apart on the page, are in fact linked together by this important, but usually invisible, line.

A single line will also give the pupil an opportunity to compose his own tune, which he can reproduce at home with ease, thereby giving him a sense of achievement. Gradually, a second line can be introduced, and a store of 'tunes' of his own can be collected. Notes at this stage can be written without stems, with the exception of minims, which need to be distinguished from semibreves to avoid confusion later on.

A second line opens up the possibility of the first five notes of the diatonic major or minor scale. By suggesting different places on the keyboard for the pupil to place his hands – using a piano keyboard picture if necessary and explaining that, like people, tunes start out from different 'homes' – the difference between the major and minor mode will be detected and can be exploited.

If you feel more comfortable teaching both treble and bass stave together with both thumbs placed on the middle C, it would reduce the visual stress on the dyslexic pupil if the top three lines of the treble stave and the bottom three lines of the bass stave were covered over. This can be done by using a typist's white ink eradicator or, more easily, by using a small frame. To make a frame, cut two identical rectangular pieces of card, 10 cm by 8 cm, and make a window 4 cm by 7 cm in each. Insert a piece of cardboard 15 cm long by 5 cm wide between the pieces of card. Stick or staple the pieces of card together down the long sides, being careful to leave enough room for the cardboard to slide freely across the middle (Figure. 4.4).

Dyslexics often have what is termed poor binocular control. Binocular control is the ability to focus the eyes together on to a single point. The added advantage of confining the reading of music to two lines only is that it can be clearly seen that, if the right-hand thumb plays the note in the space below the lower line, then the fifth finger lies on the note in the space above the upper line. The third finger will be on the note between the two lines. The same principle will apply to the left

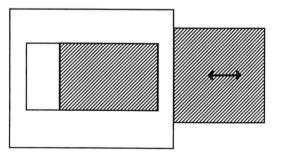

Figure 4.4

hand. On the five-line stave, it is more difficult to judge the interval of a 5th than when the 5th is illustrated on a two- or three-line stave: compare Figure 4.5a with Figure 4.5b.

Similarly with 3rds and 4ths, there are fewer distractions on the smaller stave: see Figures 4.6a and 4.6b .

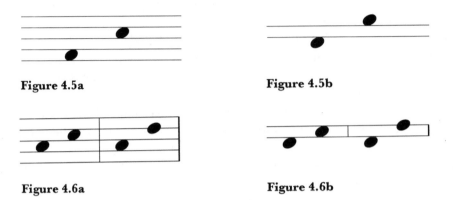

Figure 4.5a   **Figure 4.5b**

Figure 4.6a   **Figure 4.6b**

There are occasions when the notes for either the left-hand or the right-hand are written among the leger lines, but, because of the large gap between the treble and bass staves, it is not always clear how close the hands are on the keyboard. Leger lines can be confusing for anyone. How quick would you be at spotting which note is on the 5th leger line below the bass stave ? Figure 4.7a is an example of the use of leger lines being confusing.

**Alec Rowley: Fugue No. 3 from
Five Miniature Preludes and Fugues**

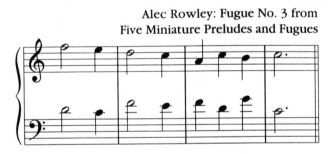

Figure 4.7a
© Chester Music Ltd. Reproduced by permission

Some composers might have chosen to write it as in Figure 4.7b. This would indeed have been clearer once the mental adjustment of the change of clef had been made. An experienced player, able to make this sort of instant adjustment, might possibly prefer it.

An easier adjustment for the inexperienced would be that employed in Figure.4.7c. This has the advantage of showing the proximity of the notes more clearly, thus showing how the two tunes relate to one another and lead-

ing the player to expect that his hands will be close to each other on the
keyboard.

What works for one pupil may not work for another, but anything is worth a try
when it comes to vexing leger lines.

Figure 4.7b
© Chester Music Ltd. Reproduced by permission

Figure 4.7c
© Chester Music Ltd. Reproduced by permission

Much research (Pavlidis and Miles, 1981) has been done and continues to be
done on factors that may upset eye function and cause added distress to a dyslexic.
It may be that the student's eye function is not disturbed so much by the parallel
lines or by poor binocular control but by the glare of black on white. The use of
tinted glasses has become accepted as an antidote to this and coincidentally an aid
to concentration.

Some publishers of music for children have addressed the problem by printing on
coloured paper. Many children react favourably to having a sheet of tinted acetate
(available from good art shops or school science laboratories) placed over the page of
music. This can be particularly helpful for the older student who has become accustomed to the stave but who is required to decipher several notes at once. Photocopying the music onto coloured paper can also be helpful, but it is always advisable to
give the pupil the opportunity to try out for himself several different shades. The
wrong colour – perhaps a bright yellow – can be counter -productive.

Another ploy that may be used is the highlighting of the stave or even the
whole system. If the next system is highlighted in a different colour, it also helps to
avoid the eyes suddenly slipping from one system to another and assists the
progression back to the left-hand side of the page.

Vertical and additional horizontal lines

In addition to the equidistant and continuous lines of the stave, there are several other lines that occur on any page of music. Some of these can cause a problem for anyone with an unreliable eye/brain relationship. Perhaps the most common of these is the stem. I have advocated the use of notes without their stems for a beginner because stems can sometimes be upsetting. It is quite common for a dyslexic to get the impression that, for example, the note in Figure 4.8a is lower than that in Figure 4.8b because the stem is reversed and appears to be 'pulling the note down'.

Figure 4.8a   Figure 4.8b

The child may need quite a lot of practice in the early stages just adding stems to notes and getting used to the look of a note with its stem going down on the left-hand side like a 'p' and up on the right-hand side like a 'd' . Because 'p's and 'd's are in themselves among the most notoriously difficult letters for a dyslexic, because of his tendency to reverse and write in looking-glass writing, it is worth taking considerable care with this. I have found it helpful to suggest that when you *lower* the stem you place it on the *left* of the note and when you *raise* the stem you place it on the *right*. It is comparatively easy to see that the middle line marks where the stems change in a scale passage from the top to the bottom of the stave. The difficulty lies with the isolated notes. If the beginner spends a minute or two every lesson familiarizing himself with the appearance of the change of orientation when the note heads cross the middle line of the stave, even before he knows what the notes are, it helps to pre-empt an optical illusory effect.

When any student has progressed to the part-playing stage, as in a Bach fugue or in many easier pieces such as the 'Five Little Preludes and Fugues' by Alec Rowley, one would probably draw attention to the direction of the stems. A dyslexic with visual problems is going to need help beyond this. It is likely that each part will have to be written out separately by the teacher so that it can be learnt as a separate entity. The same technique would apply to pieces such as 'Of Foreign Lands and People' (Schumann; Figure 4.9) in which the melody is sustained over an accompanying figure in the same hand. Colour can be used to highlight the tune, it having first been learnt from manuscript (with the correct fingering!).

You will have observed that in Figures 4.3a, 4.3b, and 4.3c I did not use any bar lines. In addition to the possibility of poor binocular control, it has been suggested (Adler-Grinberg and Stark, 1978) that some dyslexics are prone to a visual anomaly known as 'cogwheeling'. Instead of progressing smoothly from target to target, their eyes seem to 'stick' and then have to make rapid bounds (saccades) to catch up. Bar lines can act as catalysts for cogwheeling, creating a barrier between one beat and the next that can seriously disrupt the flow of the music. Many beginners' books rightly stress the importance of the first beat in the bar, but for a dyslexic it can be counterproductive to the performance of a musical phrase to draw attention to the bar lines on the page. Preferable by far is to listen to the swing of the music and do without bar lines, so that there is no potential interruption to the direction in which the eyes are moving. Again, the white eradicator comes in handy, although, unless you are very precise with your handling of this, you will have to join up the lines of the stave again afterwards, or the gaps where you have eradicated the bar lines will be almost as bad as the bar lines themselves. An alternative is to copy the tune onto manuscript paper, omitting the bar lines, provided that the copying is done very precisely.

When it comes to a double bar line with dots for a repeat, the problems that a dyslexic may have with directional confusion are compounded. Some teachers advocate the use of a coloured arrow pointing back to where the repeat begins. I have found that although this can be helpful, it creates a problem the second time round. The only thing that seems to work without causing a break in the general continuity is photocopying the repeat, carefully cutting and pasting the second time bar where it belongs so that nowhere does the eye have to perform any acrobatics.

In addition to the five lines of the stave – 10 for pianists – there are extra beams, phrase marks and ties that can add yet more lines. Sometimes, a beam can give the impression of a six-line stave, as for example in Figure 4.10.

Figure 4.9

Alternatively, a beam can have the opposite effect when it obscures one of the lines of the stave, as in Figure 4.11. In Figure 4.11, the eye has become accustomed by the end of bar 1 to reading the top line as a beam, as if the D line were the top line of the stave. In the next bar, the F line is present again, and a quick mental adjustment has to be made to judge the interval of the 4th to a G and not misread it by playing a B. What would appear to need very little visual agility for a non-dyslexic assumes much greater proportions for a pupil whose visual processing is impaired.

All the time, one searches for simplification of the page. A cluttered page – full of instructions, notes, numbers, phrasing and all that goes to represent a piece of music, especially where, for reasons of space, the printer has crowded it too closely together – can have a disastrous psychological effect on anyone. This will be multiplied several times when such a page is presented to a dyslexic. Quite often, however, the same piece of music can, with a little imagination and with the cooperation of the pupil, be transformed into something far less challenging.

Phrasing is an example of something that can quite often cause additional stress. Once the purpose of phrasing has been understood, it is usually a good idea to discuss with the pupil what simple little sign would help him to remember where the music 'breathes' and then ask him to write the sign – perhaps a little blue tick or omission mark – where it is needed. The printed phrase marks can then be erased.

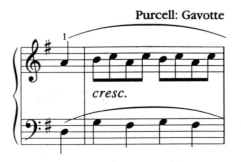

Purcell: Gavotte

Figure 4.10

Le Couppey: Pastorale

Figure 4.11

If the pupil can manage to phrase correctly without the use of the printed phrase marks, then the tie – when it arises – becomes more significant. It is still possible for someone with a short-term memory deficiency to forget why a tie is there or which note it is that has to be tied. If you cross out the tied note or write 'tie' above it or even emphasize the tie mark, which you might do for a non-dyslexic, you are actually making the page more, rather than less, difficult to read. Extra marks may excite the eye and upset the function of the brain. It is sometimes possible to keep the tie but erase the bar line to draw attention to the continuing sound, as in Figure 4.12. You can add a dot to the minim, to show that in effect it lasts for three beats, if the pupil finds this helpful. At other times, this is not feasible, as in Figure 4.13, but here the tie can be erased and a colour used to highlight the A space through the two bars, followed by the B line throughout the next two bars, and so on.

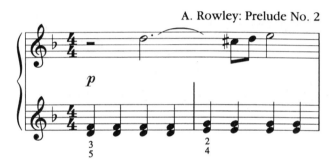

Figure 4.12
© Chester Music Ltd. Reproduced by permission

Figure 4.13
© Chester Music Ltd. Reproduced by permission

Rests, dots and accidentals

Rests can be very testing, even for non-dyslexics. It is quite common for pupils in the early stages to read the two staves separately, particularly in a passage where rests are involved. In Figure 4.14 one can see what often happens. The pupil finishes off the right-hand tune, then switches to the left-hand and either begins counting from the beginning of the bar, incorporating the minim rest – thereby creating five beats in the bar – or fails to notice any rest at all on the second beat and brings the left-hand in at least a beat early. Blocking in beats in colour through both staves, using different colours for each beat, can be a visual aid here to understanding how it all adds up to the right number of beats in the bar, but the real answer is to tackle the problem in a more multisensory way. If he can beat time comfortably, you can suggest to him that he beats time and listens while you play the tune, asking him to notice which beat is silent. Ideally, you would ask a non-dyslexic who needed help with this sort of problem to sing along with you, while beating time, but concentrating on more than one thing at a time is difficult for a dyslexic and the challenge is not worth the risk of failure.

Figure 4.14
'Grinding the Corn' from The Windmill by Leslie Fly
© 1958 Forsyth Brothers Ltd. Reproduced by permission

When a dot is used after a rest, instead of the sign for half the value of that rest, it is possible to get considerably confused. The first time that pupils meet with a dot to lengthen the value of a note by half, it is usually when they encounter a dotted minim. They learn that this means three beats. Thereafter, unless one is very meticulous about instilling the principle, they associate dots with something to do with three, or occasionally one and a half. A dyslexic tends to cling tenaciously to something he knows for sure and should not be expected to unlearn or readjust his perception of what he understood to be a fact. This means that right from the very beginning, the idea that a dot beside a note is merely adding half the value of *that note* should be firmly established. The same should apply to dotted rests, which should be practised alongside dotted notes. It only takes a moment to point out that a dotted apple would be an apple and half an apple or a dotted Mars bar would be $1\frac{1}{2}$ Mars bars. That extra half is worth having!

In Figure 4.15, the dot after the quaver rest can sometimes be ignored altogether and, because the semiquaver appears to have turned its back on the rests, it is hard to appreciate that the dot is its 'other half'. Strictly speaking, the extra beam on the first semiquaver should be facing the other way, as it is in the second beat, but the custom, as we know, is to 'tidy' the page as much as possible. This semiquaver symbol can easily be misread by someone with poor binocular control as the symbol in Figure 4.16.

Brian Chapple: Lazy Days

Figure 4.15

© Chester Music Ltd. Reproduced by permission

Figure 4.16

When the rests are supplanted by notes, as in Figure 4.17, it can be easier to understand the principle that is involved. Once this is fully understood, one can erase the rests on the score and introduce crossheaded notes in their place, thereby giving more prominence to the value of the rests, for example as in Figure 4.18. The only danger is that the pupil may see them as actual notes, in which case he may prefer to revert to the symbols for rests.

Figure 4.17   **Figure 4.18**

Nowadays, thank goodness, publishers tend not to use the old quaver rest reversed for a crotchet rest, but when one does meet it on an older piece of music, the same technique of exchanging a crossheaded note for a rest can make the reading of the rests a great deal clearer.

When one is alive to the problems that a dyslexic pupil may have with focusing or binocular control, one only has to use a little imagination to realize that, for example, a semibreve rest may be mistaken for a minim rest. Introducing numbers and counts – in the probably mistaken belief that this will help – can complicate the written page unnecessarily. We have to find ways of making the written music look as simple as possible, so that when pupils are are on their own, they are not afraid to refer to it.

At every turn, the pupil should be asked for his advice on what would help him best to understand and to remember. This strengthens the bond between teacher and pupil and personalizes the page of music for him in meaningful ways. If the teacher stamps her own personality on it, by writing on it in a way that would be helpful if she were the performer, the page will appear to the child just as alien as, or even more alien than, it did before.

One of the problems a dyslexic frequently has when learning to read is punctuation. A pupil with poor binocular control may fail to see commas and full stops altogether, thereby making nonsense of sentences. It is therefore only to be expected that when learning to read music the same should happen; he may not see the dots.

We musicians know that every dot on a page of music has a special significance of its own: we use tiny dots for staccato, repeats and to lengthen a note or a rest. The character of a phrase can be quite transformed if every dot is given its true value.

As there are examples in the works of several classical composers of the vertical wedge being used for staccato instead of the dot, it would therefore seem reasonable to use the same device for a dyslexic. This has the advantage of being easier to see, as well as having more character. The little wedge standing on its point, as if only touching the ground for an instant, seems to represent the bounce of a staccato more colourfully than does the ubiquitous dot. Alternatively, for an appreciably long passage of staccato, the picture of a bouncing ball at the beginning and a pair of hands catching the ball at the end can be enough: it all depends on the age and inclination of the pupil.

Dots for staccato can sometimes be eradicated altogether without making any difference to the character of the music. This is when they are employed as in Figure 4.19 on the final note of the slurred phrases.

Figure 4.19

The combination of phrasing and dots may arguably help a non-dyslexic to a better performance of this passage, but, if one listens to the meaning of the music, to have both is superfluous here. Anything that can muddy the page without adding anything of real value to the interpretation should be erased. Occam's razor should be one's constant companion!

There is one little dot that can easily be turned into a meaningful picture and that is the dot incorporated in the fermata. If the note to be paused on is a quiet one it adds colour to the general idea if one creates a sleeping eye ◠. Alternatively, if a loud sound is required, you can make the eye look very wide awake 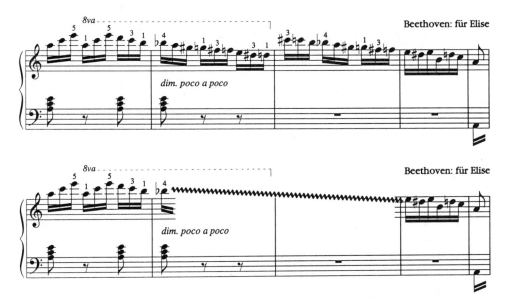. Pictures rather than hieroglyphics are often more direct in their impact.

Accidentals on the printed page cannot be avoided. During the twentieth century, there has been a move to incorporate flats and sharps into the form of the note head itself (Chailley), but this has not become widely accepted, perhaps because the sign ♯ that Chailley invented for   looks too much like a double sharp. He also used ♩ for ♭, which is hard to see. Some experimentation with the signs to help the student see that the note is to be raised or lowered is a good idea. It is distressingly common for a student to see an accidental coming somewhere and to reach for the nearest black note, whichever it happens to be. It is clear that their equilibrium has been disturbed and that they have been unable to focus on which note should be raised or lowered.

An intelligent pupil, as a dyslexic often is, can more easily understand and cope with which black note is to be expected if he has a sense of key. This immediately facilitates the playing sometimes of several bars of music at a time. It is not then necessary to highlight every sharp, flat or natural but simply to delineate the area in the new key and discuss with the pupil what distinguishing mark should be employed. There are some very musical children who sometimes associate keys with colours, e.g. yellow for A major etc., in which case a yellow highlight either above the stave or running right through between the left-hand and right-hand stave could be used. This musical approach to the problem also helps someone with an acute short-term memory deficit to remember to keep the accidental in mind throughout the bar. Once he knows why there is an accidental, it ceases to be a problem.

Chromatic scale passages are best simplified with a zig-zag line if the rhythm permits. If their complexity is causing a problem to the eyes, all but the first and last notes can be erased altogether. Compare Figure 4.20a with Figure 4.20b.

Figure 4.20a, b

Sometimes editors of students' music try to be helpful by cancelling accidentals in the next bar or even several bars later. Confusions can so easily arise with all accidentals that it is better to avoid any that are strictly unnecessary. It is a simple rule of theory that unless an accidental is repeated in the next bar, it is naturalized anyway, so the best thing to do is to erase the cancellation and simply draw attention to the rule.

Fingering

So far, everything that has been discussed has been in connection with the notes themselves and their articulation. There is, however, an added complication to the page of music and that is, of course, the numbers for fingering. We are concerned in this chapter with the dyslexic's visual problems. If he has a good aural memory but poor binocular control – finding it difficult to track steadily from left to right and to focus clearly on one thing at a time – it is easier for him to learn to feel where the next note should be than to rely on his eyes to take in numbers as well as notes. Much fingering can, and should be, erased. The place for it is in the manuscript book for practice, not on the page for performance. Fingering and phrasing really go hand in hand, and where early and eighteenth century keyboard music is concerned, it is well known that the phrasing of such music can only be understood with reference to the fingering and sometimes the grouping of quavers or semiquavers, as in Figure 4.21.

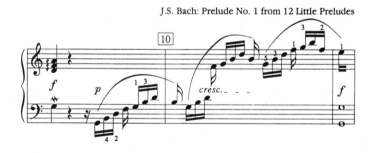

J.S. Bach: Prelude No. 1 from 12 Little Preludes

Figure 4.21

Modern European systems of fingering are designed to eliminate any undue gaps in the performance of a legato passage and to facilitate a pianistic flow that will give the performer as much freedom as possible, so that he may concentrate on interpretation. This has occasionally led, in my opinion, to slightly overpedantic recommendations.

Take, for example, the practice of changing the finger on repeated notes. The principle is undoubtedly sound in that it relaxes the muscles in the fingers, hand and arm, and thereby allows for rapid repetition without stress. Where I believe it is taken too far is where the music is only moving slowly and the note only has to be repeated once or twice. It is certainly easier to play a repeated note legato if a change of finger is employed, and it may be that the performer will feel more comfortable with a change of finger, in which case it may be written in, but it can quite often make a relatively simple passage more difficult. The dyslexic needs added security; it would seem unnecessary to advocate anything that might militate against this.

Every teacher appreciates that no two hands are the same and that what is comfortable for one may not be comfortable for another. There are accepted practices that can indeed be very helpful, for example turning the thumb under on the final note of the turn, as in Figure 4.22.

Figure 4.22

Unfortunately, from the visually aesthetic point of view, this can look extremely daunting. Ornaments are a challenge in themselves and are best written out either *in situ*, provided that an enlarged photocopy is being used, or separately in a jumbo-sized manuscript book. Is it actually necessary to add any fingering other than the original 3 – if indeed there might have been any doubt about that – and the final 1 on the last semiquaver of the turn?

Sometimes, of course, one's pupils find it easier in complicated passages to follow a string of numbers rather than a string of notes. One deprecates this because it can lead to errors in notation. However, one's whole attitude to the dyslexic is different: he has problems that we can never fully understand, and if we can help by allowing him to read numbers rather than notes for complicated corners, this is surely the best thing to do. It is, however, advisable to confine the string of numbers to the passage written out in a jumbo-sized manuscript book. There are two ways of doing this, either as in Figure 4.23a or as in Figure 4.23b.

Figure 4.23a   **Figure 4.23b**

Personally, I prefer the second way (Figure 4.23b); it seems less cluttered, but it may not suit the pupil. He may be able to think of something even better for him. In any event, he will have to learn this as a separate exercise because at speed in performance he will not have the necessary processing skills to cope. Attention can be drawn to the elongated turn shape, which is particularly clear in Figure 4.23b. When he has committed this to memory, the shape alone should be enough to trigger off the correct aural and motor response.

Tracking

If we are pianists our eye travels across the page as we read music, taking in what is written on two staves bracketed together. When we reach the extreme right-hand side of the page, we start again from the left, reading the next system down the page.

Tracking from system to system is not without its problems, and it is also quite common for a dyslexic to jump systems half way across the page. If he has this sort of problem, there are a variety of things one can do to counteract it :

1.   The music can be photocopied, and each system can be cut out and stuck onto a large piece of paper or card so that there is a much greater gap between them than is normally found on a sheet of music.
2.   Each complete system can be highlighted in a different colour.
3.   A continuous coloured line can be drawn with a highlighter between the bracketed staves. This can merge during the final bar of the system into the colour to be used for the next system.

The first suggestion is more practical when there are several other colours being used for one reason or another, but it does mean that a piece of music that nicely fitted onto the page sometimes now takes up two pages, necessitating a turn. The pupil has to decide which he would prefer.

Tracking is a crosscurricular skill. Because of the difficulties that dyslexic children frequently have with it, practice in the music lesson will pay dividends in the classroom as well. The more mature student, often working against time and with large amounts of reading to do, has to learn to scan rapidly through many pages of text. Salient points can easily be missed or misunderstood if his tracking skills are poor. It is common for a dyslexic not only to have problems with the words themselves but also often to omit words, or parts of words, altogether. The same will apply in music, particularly with repeated notes and when there is a complication of some sort either before, after or, as in Figure 4.24, both.

Figure 4.24

Poor tracking skills lead not only to omissions, but also to insertions. When a dyslexic is reading, he may slip in extra little words, plurals or suffixes. These will alter the meaning of the sentence as surely as the balance of a whole phrase will be upset if three quavers are read as four. At times, it is useful to have up one's sleeve an activity that is not directly related to the piece of music that the pupil is studying, but which is music related and which will help to strengthen his tracking skills.

Children often enjoy 'joining up the dots' to make pictures. Printed music is ideally suited for this as of course most of the time we are reading a piece of music we are mentally joining up the dots. If you are handy with a pencil and enjoy composing, you might like to try inventing some musical dot-to-dot games. First, draw a simple shape on a large five-line grid. On another piece of paper with a new grid, convert the solid line into a line of dots, add stems as you would for crotchets, add bar lines and finally place the paper inside a clear plastic envelope. Then invite the pupil to join up the dots using an overhead projector pen. The sensual satisfaction that is induced by the smooth flow of the pen over the surface of the plastic is a pleasure that often delights beyond measure. It is in strong contrast to the friction of pencil or pen on paper. The envelope has the advantage of being able to be washed clean under the tap and used over and over again. With very little of a finishing touch, either by you or by him, the line drawing can be transformed into something that he can then not only see but also play and hear (Figure 4.25).

As you play it for him again, he can trace the shape with his finger, but beware! Do not let him do it on the plastic sleeve because the ink from an overhead-projector pen comes off so easily that he will end up with no tune and very messy fingers! Unfortunately, using a plastic sleeve is not suitable for left-handers. As they draw the shape, their hand is inclined to rub out what they have just drawn. You will have to confine them to ordinary pencil and paper and you may need a photocopy of the tune so that, as you play it on the piano, they can feel the shape with their finger on the page, listening to the rise and fall of the sounds.

A musical dinosaur

Figure 4.25

This multisensory method of not only seeing and hearing a phrase, but also feeling it, is also helpful for understanding the rise and fall of the music and feeling where the climax is. It can be used for any piece of music that the pupil is learning if he is having difficulty with it.

We all know that it is more fun to be in the right than in the wrong. Another simple way to practise tracking skills and also to give the pupil an opportunity to catch his teacher 'in the wrong' is to play a very simple phrase to him incorporating a few very obvious mistakes and see if he can spot them. The mistakes can be rhythmic, melodic or dynamic. Allow him to study the phrase first to give him plenty of time to notice, for example, whether it is marked ⎯⎯ or ⎯⎯ and exactly what is happening to the tune at that point. Make it easy so that he cannot fail to notice at least one mistake. He must have the satisfaction of having found you out!

This chapter has been about specific problems that a dyslexic pupil may have when faced with a page of music and being required to use his eyes to decipher it. We do not know how each *individual* brain processes the information it receives through the eyes, but what is clear is that our brains function, in some respects, very like computers, in that thousands of connections are almost instantaneously made on the reception of information from the senses. Sometimes, also like computers, it takes a few moments for these connections to get sorted out. In order to rest the eyes and give the brain some breathing space – after a bout of intense concentration – I frequently suggest to my pupils that they go and look out of the window and count the number of different greens they can see. Green, as we know, is a restful colour. If one is teaching in an enclosed studio with no lovely view of the outside world, one can always have a poster or two on the wall or pot plants on a shelf – anything in sharp contrast to a page of music or the black and white of the keyboard. The use of this little ploy seems to be even more necessary for, and beneficial to, dyslexics. Not only does it allow time for the eyes and the brain to rest but it offers an opportunity for a change of position, which can be physically beneficial.

Summary

The whole drift of this chapter has been towards simplification and towards adjusting the score to suit the pupil. If he finds that the stave itself stimulates his brain to perceive movement of the text, then one should whenever possible erase it, or as much of it as can be dispensed with without causing confusion. Many lines, both vertical and horizontal, can judiciously be eradicated. Numbers for fingering should only be used when necessary, and dots can be reduced to a minimum. Experiments with making the score more 'user-friendly' should all be made on enlarged photocopies, and the jumbo-sized manuscript book should be at one's elbow all the time.

I have frequently advocated the use of colour. I am aware that this can be overdone. It is only too easy to have many coloured highlighters ready for every eventuality, and if one is not careful the page of music begins to look more like a kaleidoscope. The answer is, I suggest, to have several photocopies – enlarged if necessary – so that only one colour, or at the most two, is used on each copy. These should be used for practice only, unless of course the student finds that he cannot manage without the help of one of them when it comes to his next lesson. After all, it is not the piece of paper that matters but the sound of the music.

It would be too tedious for the reader if I were to enumerate every single instance of the symbolic code of music that could confuse a dyslexic with visual problems. I have attempted to give examples of the main ones, to explain why they are particularly troublesome and to suggest ways in which some of the problems can be overcome. If one is on the lookout all the time, and alive to the difficulties inherent in the music, it often needs only a little imagination to iron them out.

It should be clear by now that a dyslexic student with eye/brain coordination problems is going to find the reading of music daunting, *but it is not impossible*. The satisfaction he will get from being able to work things out for himself is immense. His sight-reading will probably always be poor, but it *does* improve. Meanwhile, he learns the skills that enable him to work out pieces of music that he has never heard before, and, when he finds that he can do this, there is sometimes no holding him. He begins to realize that he may one day become independent of his teacher. When that day comes, we know that we have done our job well.

Chapter 5
Motor problems

In this chapter, we look at the sorts of problem that a dyslexic may have with regard to motor control and coordination, with particular reference to left/right hand coordination and the hand/foot coordination needed for pedalling. Alongside and inextricably linked with coordination is the problem of left/right independence and the difficulties that arise from the dyslexic's confusion over left and right. Sometimes the degree of directional confusion does not become apparent until a later stage, when the pupil is consistently using both hands together and both similar and contrary motion coordination is required. I use the word 'coordination' to mean that particular skill which is needed when the hands play in unison, as in scales and arpeggios. Left/right independence is when the hands are required to perform different functions, as when the left hand accompanies a right-hand melody.

One of the many subtraits of dyslexia is a condition sometimes known as dyspraxia. Dyspraxia can have its own subtraits, but in general terms it means the impairment or immaturity of the organization of movement (*dys* = Greek for poor, *praxis* = Greek for doing or action). Associated with this there may be problems of language, perception and thought. The dyslexic child is not necessarily dyspraxic, nor is the dyspraxic child necessarily dyslexic, but the two conditions can go hand in hand, and it is as well to be prepared to encounter a degree of dyspraxia when teaching the dyslexic. For the purposes of this book, we will continue to use the term 'dyslexic', but, in the context of this chapter, it should be understood to mean the dyslexic *with movement or motor problems*. This is the child who is not well coordinated. He may appear to be rather clumsy and accident prone, his writing is haphazard and he finds it difficult to learn and to remember both gross and fine motor skills.

Gross motor skills can be taken to mean any movement skill that involves the whole limb, whereas fine motor skills are those which involve finger dexterity.

Balance and posture

In any field where physical agility is required, no fine motor control can be satisfactorily achieved unless the body is correctly balanced. This, I believe, is an indisputable fact. Many books have been written on the subject, and there are practitioners in techniques of all kinds, all aiming at what amounts to the same thing: a simple springboard from which individuals may soar in order to achieve their highest potential.

In the field of music, there are plenty of books and techniques to help us. Most widely recognized throughout the world today is perhaps the Alexander technique, but there are many others and all begin with relaxation. They progress in varying ways, sometimes using different, specifically designed, pieces of equipment, towards a thorough understanding of how the muscles of the body interact with one another and a consciousness of what is going on when a movement is executed, in order that the movement may be guided and controlled until it is as near perfection as possible. Ever since Robert Schumann damaged the fingers of his right hand by the excessive use of a particular device that he had invented to strengthen them, most musicians have been wary of using contraptions to build up particular muscles, but the recognition of the need to achieve a proper state of relaxation has, at any rate in the Western world, never been superseded.

The dyslexic sometimes finds it very hard to sit still. One hypothesis is that it is because a small area in the brain that is responsible for the control of the reflexes has not, in dyslexics, been fully developed. If they are told to sit still, they will only be able to do so at the expense of something else. Sitting still will, for them, involve concentration.

If a pupil is to achieve anything in the way of a performance, he will have to learn to sit straight and relaxed in order to give the utmost freedom to his arms, hands and fingers. Because intelligence is frequently not a problem, the dyslexic can often understand more readily than others that, unless he is sitting firmly on his 'sitting bones', with the soles of his feet comfortably on the floor in front of him and the weight of his spine resting on itself in a direct line from his head to his tail, he will never achieve that balance of posture which prepares the way for elegance and speed of performance.

Well-balanced posture as a prerequisite for effective tone production is common knowledge to all music teachers, yet it is surprising how many children one notices at music festivals sitting with their feet wrapped like a monkey's tail around the legs of the piano stool. If the 'normal' child has to be reminded to sit properly, how much more the dyslexic! Because he may find it exceptionally difficult to concentrate both on what he is trying to play and on how he is sitting, one has to be careful not to nag. It can be helpful to have a discussion with him about how the problem can be solved. I have found that a little picture at both the beginning and the end of a short exercise or piece can trigger the memory after a while, ensuring that the performance at least begins and ends with the player looking right, even if he slips a bit in the middle. When the child is playing without the music in front of him, he may need a gentle prod with a finger tip in the centre of his back to remind him that his posture is slipping.

If the lesson begins with the rhythmic practice described in Chapter 3, this insistence on correct posture, even while other quite bold movements are going on simultaneously, can be incorporated into the activity.

It is as well to remember that the dyslexic can tire very quickly because everything is such an effort for him. However the lesson is conducted, he should be given the opportunity to change his position frequently. He will not be able to withstand a relentless assault on his posture, even if what is being aimed at is relaxation and balance.

Gross motor control

Learning to play the piano challenges both sides of the brain to an extraordinary degree. Only the organ needs more left/right independence and coordination. The student with gross motor problems is going to have to work extremely hard, and somehow we have to find a way to lighten the load. There is no magic cure.

There is a good exercise for a cold winter day that not only sends the blood tingling into the fingertips, but also starts the brain thinking on the right lines. The child stands in the middle of the room with plenty of space all around and flings his arms across his chest so that his fingers flap loosely on to his shoulder blades behind him. As his arms cross over, he must make sure that they take it in turns to be the one on top. Twenty of those flings and I guarantee that any child arriving with cold hands will have warmed up beautifully. His brain will also have been primed so that he is more conscious of what his left and right arms are doing.

Simple hand-clapping games can also give useful stimulation to the brain; take for example the well-known playground game where two children (in our case teacher and child) stand facing one another and first clap their own hands, then their partner's right hand, their own again, partner's left, their own again and lastly both right and left together. It can be surprising to find how much concentration some dyslexics need to repeat this activity several times, and if it is varied by adding extra claps, they need to think very hard to maintain control.

It used to be the practice with ABRSM music examinations to ask the candidates to beat time in time to the music. This practice has now been dropped, but it is still a valid exercise and one that is well worth doing. Some children seem to find it exceptionally difficult, none more so than the dyslexic with gross motor problems, but if he is allowed to beat time with both arms at once, it immediately becomes much easier. This is an opportunity for playing some strongly rhythmical 'real' music to him and getting him to feel it right through his body. It is advisable to build up slowly from duple, through triple to quadruple time, making sure that the movements for each have been thoroughly assimilated before the next one is learnt. Duple time should be practised at all speeds from largo to presto, and the child should be quite clear about which is the 'down' beat before he attempts to move on to triple time and so on. As with everything else for a dyslexic, one small step at a time.

Until independence of the arms is established, it is understandable that independence of the hands will be impossible to achieve. One cannot spend the whole lesson doing exercises, but, if there appear to be reflexes in the brain that are not under control and which therefore inhibit both the coordination and the independence of the arms and hands, it is important to work on this every week. Children seem to enjoy the challenge if one sets them a little task to do at home like rubbing their tummies and patting the top of their heads. It is the sort of thing that sets the whole family off, or which can be tested on friends.

There are other simple exercises which are very valuable:

1. Raise the right arm in front of the body until the hand is shoulder high while simultaneously raising the left arm to the side of the body. Drop the arms and repeat with the left arm to the front and the right to the side.
2. Raise one arm slowly to shoulder height – either forwards or out to the side – while carrying out the same movements with the other arm at twice the speed.
3. Tap crotchets in one hand while tapping quavers in the other. Reverse the hands.
4. Tap crotchets in one hand while tapping triplet quavers in the other. Reverse the hands.

It is unwise to present too difficult a challenge to the dyslexic. He must be allowed to succeed and gradually build upon his success, giving him that confidence in himself without which there is no way forward for him. Giving him something to practise doing away from the piano, but which is ultimately going to have direct relevance to his ability to control his movements at the keyboard, is a subtle way of opening up possibilities for improvement.

Coordination for pedalling[1]

A dyslexic must have all new knowledge presented to him in a clear, systematic way, and legato pedalling is no exception.

Before any attempt is made at actually using the pedal, it will be necessary to practise another very simple exercise away from the keyboard. Not every soldier learns to march – and march in time with his fellows – with ease: sometimes it can be an extremely painful experience – literally! Feet and hands do not necessarily coordinate comfortably at all.

The child should sit with both feet squarely on the floor and his forearms and hands resting on a flat surface. The ball of the right foot is then raised, *leaving the heel on the ground*. The exercise can now begin. As the ball of the foot drops to the ground again the fingers and hands are raised from the wrist to an angle of about 45 degrees with the flat surface, whereupon the ball of the foot is lifted again as the hands drop. This see-saw movement should become quite automatic before the next step is attempted.

---

[1] I expect that many teachers teach pedalling in the same way that I do, but having observed many children at festivals dabbing at the pedals rather haphazardly, I suspect that it is not always taught very systematically.

Having made quite sure that the child is familiar with the action of the pedal and that he can manipulate it quietly with the ball of his foot, always having his heel on the ground, the following exercises should be attempted:

1.   Start with the pedal down, counting aloud slowly. No playing – just the pedal.

1	2	3	1	2	3	etc.
Up	down	hold	Up	down	hold	

2.   The same, but the teacher plays the notes of a scale, using only the index finger, on the first beat of the bar (Figure 5.1).

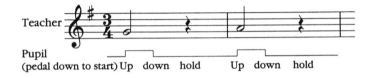

Figure 5.1

3.   The same again, but the pupil puts the pedal down immediately after releasing it on the first beat of the bar. It may be necessary to count 1 and 2 and 3 and, etc. and depress the pedal on the 'and' (Figure 5.2).

Figure 5.2

4.   This time the teacher holds the index finger of the pupil and guides him to do the playing. This will need a great deal of practice before proceeding to:
5.   The pupil plays unaided, still counting slowly.

Fine motor control

For those who are not good at controlling their fingers – those whose writing is probably very poor, whose pencil grip is tight and awkward and who, in more technical terms, have poor fine motor control – there is a great deal to be said for practising away from the keyboard as well as at the keyboard. Some children, with little in the way of problems, quickly tire of practising passages on the keyboard lid or on a table: they want to feel the keys beneath their fingers and to make the sounds happen. But the dyslexic, on the other hand, often enjoys 'dumb' practice because he knows that the chances of 'getting it right' when he eventually transfers this practice to the keys themselves is very much higher. Any mistakes he may have made in practice have not been audible, and the goal is achieved in what seems a much shorter time. It gives his confidence a real boost.

Every teacher tries to present new information as clearly as possible and in a way that will be meaningful to the pupil, but however clearly and thoroughly introduced it is, it may still take time – very little time or considerably longer according to the sophistication of the machinery with which the child has been endowed – for the brain to assimilate it before it can be reproduced. Most children nowadays are computer literate, and they understand that if you feed some information into a computer, it takes a little while for that information to be processed. They react well to the suggestion that they will have to give their brains time to process information, in whatever form it is presented. The symbol of the egg-timer on the computer screen is one to which they can relate.

I have mentioned before (Chapter 4) the beneficial effect of a rest for the eyes. The rest can also be of value to the muscles in the fingers and hands. On returning to the keyboard after a change of scene, the result is often an unerring performance of the passage that has just been under consideration, provided that some really hard work had gone into it before the rest. The rest need not be long: perhaps long enough to ask him what he had for breakfast, or how he played in the match on Saturday – *anything* unconnected with crotchets and quavers! Explain to him that you are allowing time for his brain-computer to get itself sorted out. Then when time is up, it is worthwhile rehearsing once what is to be done before attempting a performance. If his brain has not sent the correct messages to his fingers during rehearsal – if it is clear that yet more work is needed – then leave it for another week. Do not risk failure and do not suggest to him that he practise it on his own unless you are *absolutely* sure that he knows what to do.

Much training of the brain-to-muscle pathway can be done with the eyes closed. This seems to concentrate the energy and channel it into the fingers. When the child is working at something with his eyes watching what his fingers are doing, it is sometimes almost as if he were trying to guide his fingers by his eyes. That is not using his tactile sense to the extent it could be used: the learning is still not being done multisensorily. With his eyes closed, he is concentrating fully on how it feels, and all his energy is channelled into the movements of his fingers and their relationship with the keys.

There is another spin-off from practising with the eyes closed besides an increased awareness of how a particular passage should feel. In his imagination, the child is visualizing what the keyboard looks like as he is manipulating his fingers. This extra aid to familiarity with his instrument is another little brick in the building of the edifice. Elements in a motor sequence overlap in time. A man walking down the street is transferring the weight of his body first onto one foot and then onto the other in one smooth progression. Similarly, when a pianist executes a scale passage, the second finger must already be moving towards its position before the first finger is released. It is essential that he has an inner picture of the keyboard, directly linked to his fingers. The lack of inner picture is what often contributes to the inability of some children to progress.

There is a curious anomaly here where dyslexics are concerned. Their picture is not necessarily the same as our picture. We see a pattern of black notes on white that is consistent from one end of the keyboard to the other. Some dyslexics are more graphic than others in describing what they see, but it is sometimes obvious that their perception of the keyboard is more uneven than this. They know that the pattern is consistent, but to them it feels different, and it is sometimes worth discussing with them how it feels so that both teacher and pupil are on the same wavelength.

Hand independence

The ability to play contrapuntal music well must be one of the heights to which many a musician aspires but fails to reach. To delineate clearly the strands of a Bach fugue, for example, requires enormous concentration and control of touch and tone, which is difficult enough for anyone. There are, however, many instances of simple part-playing – the preliminary to counterpoint – to be found in much music that is not contrapuntal. Over and over again, right from the first pieces that children learn, one meets with the need for the player to be able to release a note or chord in one hand in order to play the same note or chord again, while the other hand maintains a legato passage.

Even quite talented children may have difficulty with this at first, but a dyslexic will find it exceptionally hard. His hands appear to have an invisible thread tying them together so that what is done with one hand causes a mirror reaction in the other. Initially, he needs an exercise in which one hand plays on every beat of the bar while the other hand only plays on alternate beats, for example Figure 5.3. This is then inverted so that the roles of the hands are reversed. He must make sure to lift the resting hand clear of the keys at first until he is quite familiar with the sensation. Gradually, he may reduce the amount of lift until his fingers only float to the top of the key as sufficient weight is released to enable the key to return to its resting position.

The refinement of this exercise is when both techniques – legato in one part with repeated notes in another – are confined to one hand only (Figure 5.4). The uninitiated will lift both hands at the end of bars 1 and 2, creating a stilted and breathless performance of this gentle little tune, which lies under the hands well. In order to counteract this, the child must first listen carefully to a demonstration of the smooth phrase that he is trying to emulate.

The next step is to work on the left-hand chords as in Figure 5.5, making sure that the thumb can be seen to lift on the last quaver of the bar. This is another instance in which practice on the keyboard lid first is the quicker way to success. It should also be practised 'blind', listening for the legato line and being conscious of the lifted thumb.

Figure 5.3

Müller: Melody in F

Figure 5.4

Figure 5.5

Finally, the right-hand can be added, but only one bar at a time, pausing on the final quaver and allowing the left thumb to continue sounding until that moment, as in Figure 5.6.

Figure 5.6

This technique is one that should be learnt very early on. It will have to be practised many times until it can be done in many different forms, and therefore the earlier it is done the better. If it is not done early on, later, when the child wants to play faster, his ear may well have become lazy and it is hard for a teacher to insist on what may seem a small item of technical expertise, but one which nevertheless makes all the difference to the sense of the music.

The same mental process underlies the technique needed for a passage that is legato in one hand but staccato in the other.

Motor response to rhythmic symbols

In the English language, there are several basic words – for example 'and', 'the', 'he', 'she', 'they', 'on', 'in', 'of' – that children soon learn to read at a glance because of the frequency with which they occur. They take in the whole word at one gulp, as it were, without recourse to the phonetics involved. The sight of the word is enough to initiate the correct response. A dyslexic child will be able to recognize and read a fair number of short words, even though he may have considerable difficulty with longer ones. In music, it is not possible to draw any exact parallels, but the principle of learning through frequent repetition is one that we can adapt with the use of flashcards. I have two sets of basic rhythms on flashcards. Set 1 consists of the 10 cards shown in Figure 5.7.

Figure 5.7

My flashcards are coloured pale green, but any restful colour would do. They measure 15 cm by 21 cm. The notes themselves are written in black and stand approximately 6 cms high. I hold up card number 1 for the child to see for about 4 seconds while I quietly count 1 2 1 2 at MM 60, and then ask the child to clap from memory what he has seen, including the repeat. If he gets it right, we go on to another card, keeping the beat continuous with quiet – sometimes whispered – counting. The more experienced the child, the faster one can go and the greater the number of cards that can be used.

Having got used to this activity, one can invite *the child* to select the cards and do the counting, reversing the roles. What he has to do now is to judge whether the clapping that he has heard is correct, and of course one purposely includes several mistakes, which he enjoys spotting. Again, as with many activities, it is inadvisable to go on for too long, but it is more interesting than clapping a whole line of rhythm, which is often expected in early primers and sight-reading books, and it has the element of a game about it. Success is also more achievable, because of the brevity of the exercise and because of the lack of interference from any other written material.

Set 2 of the flashcards is pale blue. It is in triple time and incorporates rests. To indicate the rest, the pupil has to put his fingers to his lips. This set is much more testing, so, in order to ensure that the pupil does not fail, I do not expect him to memorize what is on the card. He gets a count of 3 from me and then claps or taps the rhythm on the card.

It is quite common for a dyslexic to feel uncomfortable with triple time, so he may need some preliminary whole-body exercise before he can manage this set. For example, he may profit from walking round the room, counting 1–2–3, clapping on every first count with big, bold arm movements.

There are, of course, countless different rhythms one could choose. With older children and in order to practise more sophisticated rhythms, one can draw a rhythm 'clock' (Figure 5.8), using the rhythmic patterns that the pupil has met before but which may not yet produce in him an automatic response. This clock can be used for a 'follow my leader' exercise.

Figure 5.8

The exercise goes like this:

1.   The teacher establishes a slow, steady pulse (e.g. ♩ = MM 60) by tapping the
      crotchet in the centre of the circle several times.
2.   The pupil joins in, clapping in time with the teacher's tapping.
3.   Keeping the pulse beat going, the teacher varies the rhythm to be clapped
      by the pupil by pointing to one of the rhythmic patterns round the clock.
      She then points back to the crotchet in the centre for the next beat.
4.   The pupil follows suit by attempting to clap the rhythmic pattern that the
      teacher has chosen. If he has any difficulty with remembering how to clap
      it, the teacher can tap it out as she points to it, repeating the process until he
      can manage on his own.
5.   The teacher, having first pointed to the central crotchet beat, continues to
      alternate pointing at the chosen rhythmic pattern with pointing to the
      central crotchet until the pupil can easily switch from beat to pattern.
6.   The teacher selects another rhythmic pattern, which the pupil copies by
      clapping, and so on until all the rhythms are incorporated and the pupil can
      clap any one at will.

Children with good spatial aptitude and good visual memory can quite quickly
become used to the relative position of each rhythmic pattern on the clock. It is
therefore important to vary the positions so that the child is obliged to examine
the content of the pattern and not merely rely upon its position on the clock.
   The same idea can be adapted for use in compound time.
   This kind of rhythmic practice is beneficial for the dyslexic who needs the same
piece of information presented to him in as many ways as possible in order to
discover the one that is really going to strike home. His brain does not work in the
logically connected way in which other children's brains work. We have to present
new ideas in all sorts of different ways, and then we have to reinforce them with
constant revision. The use of rhythm flashcards for this purpose becomes an activity that the pupil recognizes and that gives him confidence. It can also, if it is judiciously used, relieve the tension of trying to marry rhythm and notes – a rhythmic
and motor response – into the performance of a piece of music.

Spatial aptitude

It will be a familiar scene to many a piano teacher: the child who comes into the
room looking cheerful and friendly and then, seated on the piano stool, takes
three times as long as other children actually to get his hands on to the keyboard
and begin. One wonders why he is so slow. Has he not practised? Some children,
of course, have not practised, and then one gets the excuses, but some protest that
they have. If this slowness to get going persists, one can be sure that there is a
genuine problem and that it is possibly one of lack of spatial ability, probably
combined with poor motor coordination.
   Directional confusion – the uncertainty that a dyslexic may have regarding the

left and right sides of his body (see Chapter 1) – may account for much of the general disease that the dyslexic sometimes appears to have with his own body. There does, however, seem to be some other factor, or factors, that aggravates the situation. It has been observed that dyslexics sometimes have a poor perception of space. They find it difficult to judge distances, which would account for simple things like hesitancy when stepping off a bus, or, conversely, misjudging the depth of the step and falling over, thereby contributing to the reputation for being accident-prone. They also find recognizing shapes and patterns difficult, which will apply both to patterns on the score and patterns on the keyboard.

Programmes have been developed to help children with poor spatial ability, and it is claimed (Ayres, 1979 and Lefroy, 1990) that this also improves their literacy, particularly their writing. Exercises have been developed to stimulate those parts of the brain that appear to be malfunctioning.

Many teachers begin every lesson with some form of technical preparation, and any child who is taking a long time to get accustomed to the keyboard needs the assurance that familiar exercises give to him. Several primers introduce simplified versions of the well-known Hanon exercise (Figure 5.9).

Once this has been mastered, it is often abandoned in favour of something else, but Hanon's original intention was that it – and the other versions that follow in his book – should be learnt in all keys and at increasing speeds. This can be immensely valuable as a way of getting to know the keyboard and keys other than C major without adding the complication of a different finger patterning. Each exercise in the original continues for two octaves, ascending and descending; I would suggest that for a dyslexic child one octave might be enough. It should also be practised in each hand separately.

Every time a new key is introduced, the exercise should be transposed into that key and relearnt. This means that the thumbs will have to become familiar with playing the black notes, but, although the practice may go against the grain for those brought up in the Matthay school, think of the advantages! Not only are the sound and shape of the new key thoroughly reinforced, but when the hand is placed over the keyboard, so that the thumbs can conveniently reach the black notes, the fingers become really intimate with the keys. New finger patterning does not have to be learnt each time – this is kept for the scale and arpeggio alone – so the load of new information is kept to the minimum.

Figure 5.9

There are plenty of other useful exercises that can be used in the same way and the inventive teacher will make up her own as well, often using an awkward passage in a piece as the basis for a short exercise. Here (Figure 5.10) is one that developed from a passage in a piece where my pupil James had to put the fourth finger of his right hand next to his thumb.

Figure 5.10

Familiarity, then, brings reassurance, and repetition builds muscle tone and enables better coordination. Moreover, a change of key rests and relaxes the ear so that repetition need not be a tedious experience either for the pupil or the teacher.

Fingering

If you ask a dyslexic first to put his hand behind his back and then to tell you which of his fingers you touch, it would not be uncommon to find that he is unable to do so with any conviction. Many can, proving that messages from the finger to the brain are correct, but even these dyslexics frequently have more difficulty with sending messages from the brain to the correct finger than does the non-dyslexic.

It is quite common for a left-handed dyslexic to reverse the order of finger numbers in the left hand. He may automatically think of his little finger, which the non-dyslexic knows as his fifth finger, as finger number 1. What we read as 5 4 3 2 1, he may read as 1 2 3 4 5. Until the teacher is aware of what is happening, it is easy to think that he is not concentrating, but when she realizes that he not only has to remember which numbered finger he has to play but also that the number he thinks of is not the same as the number his teacher is thinking of, it is a great deal easier to be sympathetic.

A most valuable piece of advice, given to me by a teacher of dyslexics, was 'Write on his fingers'. Soft felt-tip ink washes off fairly easily and, provided he agrees to it – which children usually do in this age of face-painting – it can help enormously towards reminding a pupil which finger is which. Another way to avoid confusion by calling out the number of the finger to be used is simply to touch the finger.

A problem often arises with dyslexics whose first instrument is a stringed instrument where the finger numbering is different. The index finger is 1 for the violin instead of 2, as it is for the keyboard. Here too, visible numbers on the fingers can be of considerable assistance until the right reaction is instantaneous. Ultimately, every player has to know instinctively which finger is which, but that happy situation may take a dyslexic longer to achieve.

In order to go some of the way towards solving this problem, I now invariably start all beginners off with a simple exercise that I call 'crab-walking' (Figure 5.11).Those with no particular problems soon grow out of it, having learnt two valuable lessons:

1. that the hand must be held high enough to enable free passage of the thumb underneath;

2. that in order to pass the thumb underneath, all that is needed is a little rotary tilt of the wrist.

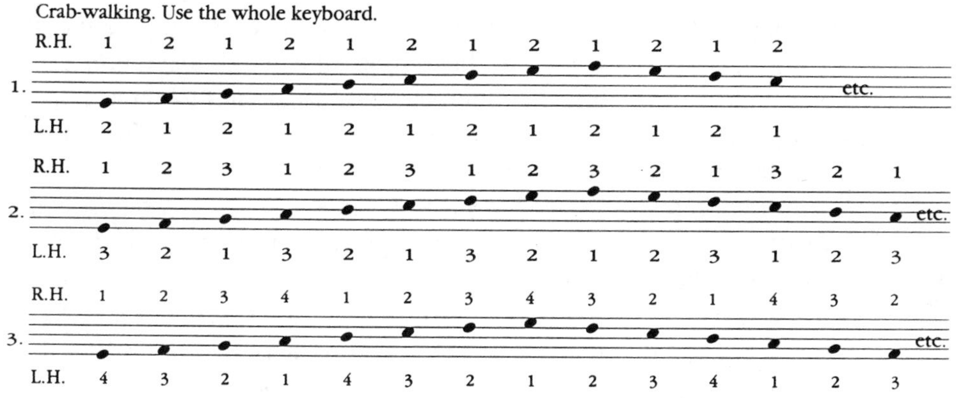

Crab-walking. Use the whole keyboard.

Figure 5.11

The dyslexic, however, may need to continue with the exercise for many weeks, getting his fingers sorted out. Any finger game is good if it encourages better familiarity with the fingers. Crab-walking is a finger game that also has the advantage of lending itself to practice on any flat surface. It can also be used in a variety of ways to establish the principle of fingering for scales, long before their formal introduction.

Besides learning 1 and 2 above, crab-walking reinforces his perception of travelling up and down the keyboard with both left and right hands and getting his ears accustomed to listening for evenness of touch. It gives him an opportunity to experience the lowest and highest sounds, and it encourages him to cross his hands well across his body. Some musically talented dyslexics have been known to continue into adulthood having severe difficulties with this. Not only do they feel uncomfortable moving across the midline of their bodies, but also associating the right hand with a tune or isolated notes in the bass while the left hand maintains an accompaniment in the middle range – or vice versa – is something that may need many hours of dedicated practice. Every new concept is best introduced simply at first, as every teacher knows, and I believe that the crab-walking exercise assists as a first introduction to the low sounds being played by the right hand, or high sounds by the left hand.

However much talent one has, as Rubinstein once said to a gathering of students that included Tobias Matthay at the Royal Academy of Music, 'real *hard work* is the only road to success'. The dyslexic just has to work that much harder.

Scales

It is the custom to teach the scale of C major first on the keyboard. It is certainly the easiest to play with separate hands. In the circle of the keys (from no sharps in the key signature through to seven sharps and back down the flats until there are none left), it is the cornerstone. It is the first scale in piano examinations for all the most widely recognised schools of music. It also follows on quite well from crab-walking. The only trouble about it is that the moment the 'hands together' stage is reached, it is one of the most difficult. There are no black notes to act as a focus for the fingering, and even fairly advanced non-dyslexic students can trip up when they are expected to play four octaves up and down fast.

There are valid arguments for starting with C major, but there are also valid arguments for starting at the other end of the spectrum if the pupil is dyslexic. Assuming that a scale book for an examination is not being used, and that scales are being learnt from memory as an aid towards technical expertise, there can be other points of departure that may ultimately be more helpful than starting with C major. If any one of the scales that incorporate all the black notes is chosen – Db (enharmonic C♯), F♯ or B major – not only is familiarity with the pattern of the black notes encouraged and the feel of them introduced, but also, at the hands-together stage, the thumbs play the same notes. Fingering is therefore a great deal easier. It could be argued that pieces in these keys are not written for beginners, and that if simultaneous theory work is being done, it involves writing a huge key signature at the beginning. This is true. On the other hand, one has to decide which is the most important thing for a dyslexic pupil. As all scales are learnt and performed from memory anyway, thereby dispensing with the urgency of learning how to write them down or to read them from score (which for a dyslexic is another problem altogether, see Chapter 7), I suggest that the advantage of learning the feel of both black and white notes together and how the keyboard is laid out is well worth considering.

The trouble with C major is that all the white notes look and feel the same. The semitones E–F and B–C look just like the tones, and the kinaesthetic link between the feel and the sound of a major scale may not be clear for some people. On the other hand, both B major and Db major encourage the kinaesthetic link. The semitones can be easily felt as well as heard. Not only that, but the hand has to be held higher to play the black notes, thereby facilitating the passage of the thumb underneath and encouraging a better position and more even tone.

Black notes can so easily be regarded as enemies. Unless a child has learnt to enjoy playing them from a very early stage, he is likely to give up learning altogether when he is expected to cope with more than about three or four in the key signature. The dyslexic may well give up earlier unless the black notes have been his friends from the start.

The logical 'handfuls' of black notes can be clearly demonstrated and used in the black note scales. B major for example can be practised as in Figure 5.12.

Finally on this subject, the difference between sharps and flats can be pointed out. B major scale starts on a white note and has sharps. D♭ major starts on a black note and has flats. Children introduced in the conventional way to scales with flats in the key signature often do not realize that F major is the only one that starts on a white note. They frequently do not understand that the reason why a black note is sometimes called a flat is because it lowers a note a semitone and is sometimes called a sharp because it raises a note a semitone. Singing the letter names of the notes of the scale should be encouraged as much and as early as possible to help with this difficulty.

If it can be arranged for both hands to feel as similar as possible on the keyboard, fingering should be altered accordingly. It is obviously impossible much of the time, but, for instance, there is no reason why F major scale should not start with the third finger in the left hand. At the hands-together stage, both fourth fingers can then play the B♭. An adjustment has to be made at the top, the left-hand playing top F with the third finger, but far from being a hindrance, I have found this helpful for my dyslexic students who have found it difficult to remember to stop at the top on the fourth finger of the right-hand. The very fact that their attention has been diverted to the left hand has been of assistance and the rest of the scale has fallen neatly into place.

This particular fingering for the F major scale may not be at all helpful to some dyslexics. It was originally worked out with one pupil who seemed to need a more definite point of reference in each octave than the conventional fingering allows. The fourth fingers playing together on the B♭s created the point of reference he needed.

It is helpful to establish a few ground rules for any student struggling with the fingering of scales. These may be a real lifeline for a dyslexic. In fact, he is unlikely to be able to manage without them. For example the basic system demands that, except in exceptional circumstances – such as the left hand bottom note of B major/minor or the right hand top note of F major/minor – the fourth finger of each hand only plays once in each octave. If, therefore, the position of the fourth

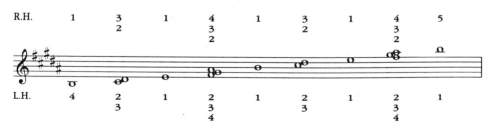

Figure. 5.12

finger is pinpointed for every scale, the rest should follow without any question. There are a few other rules that can save a lot of time if they are pointed out right from the beginning:

1.   If the keynote is a white note, the thumbs in both hands will play it, except at the top or the bottom.
2.   In all the major scales with flats, the fourth finger of the right hand *always* plays B♭.
3.   In all major scales with sharps, up to a maximum of five (the number of fingers on one hand), the fourth finger of the right hand will be on the nearest black note below the keynote. (The term 'leading-note' can be introduced very early.) The same rule applies to all harmonic minor scales beginning on a white note except for C and F, which have no immediate black note a semitone below the keynote.
4.   All major scales beginning on a flat, up to a maximum of five, begin with the fingering 3 2 1 4 in the left hand. Both 3 and 4 will fall on a black note.
5.   In all arpeggios where there is a mixture of black and white notes, the thumb of the left hand falls on the highest white note in the group, whereas the thumb of the right hand falls on the lowest.

In most books of scales, the suggestion is made that the fingering at the beginning of scales that begin on black notes should be altered slightly in the right hand from the fingering that is used at the next octave. I would eschew this idea. In my experience, it is far better to be totally consistent throughout. Consistency helps to establish the rules. To burden a dyslexic with too many rules defeats the object of making things as clear as possible, but those that are most helpful should not in any circumstance be waived.

A child with poor spatial aptitude can sometimes be helped to learn the notes of his scales and arpeggios by placing coloured markers such as tiddlywinks, which can be easily moved about, on the keys. It is not advisable to use adhesive paper dots unless one is demonstrating on a dummy keyboard or piano picture. The other markers that peel off the keys cleanly are those small circular Velcro stickers one can buy at any haberdashery counter.

The notes of the scale, or whatever is to be learnt, can be marked out on the keyboard, perhaps using red markers on the white notes and yellow markers on the black. The pupil can even work out for himself, using his knowledge of the diatonic major scale, where to put the markers. The pattern is 'frozen' on the keyboard. The child then plays the scale, hands separately, an octave higher or lower than where the markers are but keeping his eyes on the markers and feeling his way with his fingers.

The harmonic minor scale can be learnt by simply moving the third and sixth counters of the major scale down a semitone, remembering to change the colour from red to yellow if necessary. More exciting still is when the descending melodic scale is learnt and the link with the relative major can be clearly seen.

A similar idea, using a representation of the black and white keys incorporated into the writing of the music, has been used for some time by one experienced teacher of dyslexics. He uses the beam as an indication of a 'handful' of notes and writes the scale as in Figure 5.13. Where the beam slopes, the hand has to be ready to move on up or down. When the beam is horizontal, the hand stays still. No fingering is used because the 'handful' idea renders fingering unnecessary. The pupil is expected to count the number of notes beamed together and choose the appropriate finger. It is a system that works well when a pupil is left on his own to practise a scale and needs a reminder of how to work it out.

Figure 5.13

Broken chords and arpeggios

For the dyslexic child, who is often cramped and inhibited in his movements, arpeggios can be a wonderful way of finding release from this inhibition and experiencing the freedom and musical satisfaction that the keyboard can offer.

Even children who are not necessarily going to take any formal examination enjoy being able to sweep up and down the keyboard. They like to cover as much ground as possible, making the piano resonate from bass to treble and back again. It sounds difficult. It gives the player a feeling of power and is a great confidence-builder. Which one of us has not done it and felt the better for it?

The conventional place to start is with C major, but is this the best place for a dyslexic? I believe that arpeggios should be enjoyed for themselves: for the sound they make, for the tactile pleasure they can give and for their value in establishing a knowledge of the geography of the keyboard.

The easiest arpeggio to play is surely B major. It lies under the hands with the longest and strongest fingers on the two black keys, and the swing under for the thumb is facilitated by this. The black keys are easy ones to find, being situated on either side of the 'gap', and even playing hands together is relatively easy because the fingering is as near a match as possible. In fact I like to start with the hands together for one octave in contrary motion, using the pedal, and allow the child to cover several octaves as in Figure 5.14.

The dynamics help not only to create a more musical effect, but also to develop lateral freedom of the wrist. Once the hand position has become really familiar, there are all sorts of different ways in which this basic exercise can be varied, and it is only a small step to playing in similar motion and eventually to a continuous arpeggio.

Progressing from B major arpeggio, there are two natural choices:

1.   The group that contains E♭, A♭, D♭ major and C♯, F♯, G♯ minor; and
2.   B♭ minor.

Figure 5.14

Although it may seem quite out of context, I favour B♭ minor because of the
natural way the hand lies over the keys and also because it is so refreshing to have a
change to the minor mode! The rearrangement of the major and minor 3rds in the
triad can be so clearly seen here and the darker character of the chord demonstrated. It obviously cannot be taught in quite the same way with hands together but
as an exercise in covering the keyboard with one sweep of the hand, it is invaluable.

The arpeggios listed in group 1 above also lie under the hands well and
encourage the child to appreciate the delights that the keyboard, with its particular configuration of black and white keys, has to offer. The pedal can be used
freely, and dynamics should be varied as much as possible. Rhythms can be varied
too, but it is advisable not to introduce numbers into the activity by counting
aloud the beats in the bar – they can be mistaken for a fingering instruction.
Words work much better, besides having more character, e.g. Figure 5.15 (with
apologies to Lewis Carroll and Edward Lear):

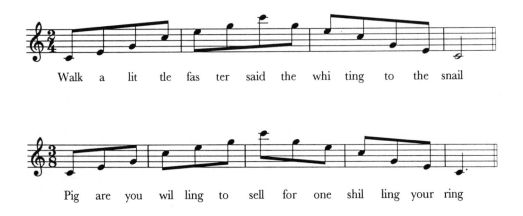

Figure 5.15

Research indicates that the addition of language cues makes rhythm pattern discrimination and performance easier for children between the ages of 7 and 9 (Atterbury, 1985). Those of us who have used words to help pupils with tricky rhythms know that the practice can be helpful far beyond the age of 9.

There comes a moment when fingering really is essential, and this is another instance in which numbers written on the fingers can be a great help. It can also be useful to have a life-size keyboard picture handy on which can be stuck the little circular stickers one can buy in any good stationery shop. A sticker with a finger number on it can be stuck on the appropriate key on the picture, and the pupil can take this home with him as an *aide-mémoire*. A different colour can be used for each hand. It is a good idea to make a photocopy of the keyboard picture and slide two pictures, back to back, one for each hand, into one clear plastic sleeve. The arpeggio can then be practised on any flat surface, and the picture remains intact. Unfortunately, an A4 sleeve is only large enough to encompass a 12th on a keyboard but this is still enough to cover the first octave and set the pattern going for the second octave, thereby helping with the most difficult areas.

Broken chords can be divided between the hands as shown in Figure 5.16. This gives the child an opportunity to learn to plan the next movement of each hand while the other one is playing. Because the next movement is an exact replica of what he has just performed two octaves lower, part of the problem is already solved for him: he knows what it is going to feel like. Now he has to concentrate on finding the new place and, driven by the speed he sets himself, his ear encourages him to think ahead as well as he is able. First and second inversions of the chord can be treated in the same way (Figure 5.17 and Figure 5.18).

Figure 5.16

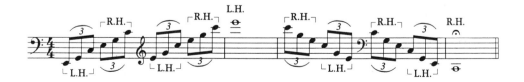

Figures 5.17

Figure 5.18

Summary

Learning to play a musical instrument is an occupation that demands a high degree of physical coordination, which the dyslexic with motor problems, poor spatial ability or directional confusion is going to find difficult to develop. He will have to begin by learning to be more at ease with his own body, which will entail concentration on sitting well and trying to maintain a relaxed but well-balanced posture. We have to be realistic, though: for some this may be literally impossible. All we can hope for is the right balance at moments when there is nothing else on which he has to concentrate, namely the beginning and the end of his performance.

Physical exercises and games can stimulate the brain towards better gross motor control, without which there will be little hope of fine motor control. Fingers that will not respond to order may benefit from practice away from the keyboard and particularly from 'blind' practice, which enhances the kinaesthetic experience.

Because it is so difficult for a dyslexic to concentrate on more than one thing at a time, it is useful for him to have a limited store of rhythmic patterns in his brain, that, on sight, produce the appropriate physical response. Flashcards can be used for this.

There is huge scope on the piano for making wonderful sounds, even for the beginner. The conventional emphasis on starting by learning the white notes could surely be re-examined in the light of what we know about dyslexics. A child with spatial aptitude problems can be encouraged to enjoy the freedom and excitement of the keyboard by integrating the black notes into his playing right from the start.

The use of the sustaining pedal can also be encouraged from very early on, but only to sustain arpeggios or broken chords. Real legato pedalling needs a strict systematic approach to ensure that hand/foot coordination is a well-rehearsed, conscious activity.

Coping with 10 fingers and two hands can be quite a tall order for a dyslexic who has not established the relationship between left and right. He can be helped in the first instance, by numbers written on his fingers but he will need repetition of simple exercises such as 'crab-walking' until the correct reaction to a finger instruction is automatic. The basic principles underlying the fingering of scales and arpeggios should then be instilled so that each one is not learnt in isolation from the rest. Adhering to a few rules that are never broken makes the whole process far easier, although it may be possible to adjust some scale fingering to meet the special needs of a pupil.

For consideration

Since the 1950s, scientists have had the necessary techniques for measuring developments in brain structure as a result of giving a subject – usually an animal such as a rat or a dog – opportunities to develop its senses and movements in an enriched environment. It has been found that the enriched environment resulted in healthier brains, more interconnections between neurones and a greater ability to learn and perform a task.

Experimenters in widely scattered centres throughout the world have been working on the proposition that, if animals can improve their brain function by reaction to a physically enriched environment, the child who is malfunctioning in the area of language and speech because of an insufficiently well-organized brain may then also benefit from a physically enriched environment. There have been studies on the effects of an extensive program (sic) of, among other things, easy listening games, dancing, marching and walking in pace with syllables for stimulating phonological (literally, the sounds of words) awareness in preschool children (Lundberg et al., 1988).

No significant effect was observed on functional linguistical skills, such as comprehension of oral instructions or vocabulary, nor did it affect the learning of letter names, but there were significant effects on some other linguistic skills. For example, small but significant effects were observed on rhyming tasks, which is where dyslexics often fail, and also on tasks involving word and syllable manipulation. Further to that, and much more dramatic, were the effects on the phonemic tasks, that is to say, tasks involving the smallest sounds made by the letters of the alphabet. The children who had undergone the programme, which had used, among other things, music and movement to stimulate their listening skills, had a clear advantage when it came to learning to read. This advantage persisted. Lundberg et al. claim that their data offer some obvious and promising practical implications for the prevention and remediation of reading failure.

Chapter 6
Memorizing and sight reading

A dyslexic musician who was the holder of a demanding position as a music adviser told me that he achieved his Licentiate of the Royal Academy of Music on the piano because he was awarded such high marks on his performance of his rehearsed pieces – which he performed from memory – that his failure on the sight-reading section was relatively immaterial. This must be the sort of experience that many a dyslexic musician will recognize. I suspect that the same imbalance of skills also applies to many students who find either memorizing or sight-reading difficult and therefore concentrate their energies on areas in which they are likely to excel. Improvement in weak areas is often, for anybody, a matter of practice: hours and hours of practice. The dyslexic student may be considerably daunted by the thought of having to give so much time to the aspect of practising that he finds most difficult and enjoys the least of all. However, if we consider in some depth what is involved in both memorizing and sight-reading, it may be possible to evolve a fresher approach to these subjects, which will make that practising more meaningful and therefore more rewarding.

Memorizing and sight-reading are both activities that rely on functions of the memory, which is why I have chosen to consider them side by side. This chapter contains a brief description of some aspects of memory, with particular reference to the sensory memory required for the performance of any piece of music. This is followed by a consideration of the problems that anyone may encounter with sight-reading and how these may be compounded for a dyslexic.

Much research has been done on the subject of memory. I am aware that the following descriptions may seem much oversimplified to the experts in this field, but I believe that it is necessary to shed *some* light on how the memory works in order to stimulate music teachers into thinking more positively about how they may approach the subjects of memorizing and sight-reading, particularly and specifically when dyslexic pupils are concerned.

Although it is possible to find niches in the music profession where either memorizing or sight-reading can be avoided, it must be understood that for the aspiring professional musician, who hopes to find a place in an orchestra or a choir, an ability to sight-read is of vital importance. While offering some ideas that may help the musician who has particular difficulties in this area, it would be wrong to hold out any false hopes that might engender unrealistic expectations and lead to disappointment.

I will conclude with some suggestions for helping to overcome these difficulties.

Memory

There is a widely held view of memory that is known as the 'identity theory'. This suggests that memory cannot be understood as long as we continue to think of it as a 'mental ghost in the physical machine' (Warnock, 1987). Baroness Warnock believes that mental events and events in the brain are in some sense the same happening. I take this to mean, when restricted to the field of instrumental music, that if we create a musical memory by using our fingers on the keyboard, the creation of it – the aesthetic pleasure that it gives us – the sound of it in our ears – the feel of it in our fingers – and the meaning it has for us in our musical soul – are all facets of that same memory. We cannot relive one side alone: all have contributed to the whole to a greater or lesser degree, and the whole has become part of our 'identity'.

It has been pointed out, however, that the laboratory view of memory is likely to remain the major source of theoretical development (Baddeley, 1990). This divides memory into various interlinking components or subsystems. These include:

1. the initial information store;
2. some sort of short-term memory (which may have several different features and be known by other names, such as 'working memory' or 'buffer store');
3. long-term memory, which can be divided into memory for events and experiences (episodic memory) or for the meaning of words or concepts (semantic memory).

Information in the initial information store decays within less than 1 second (see p.99). The short-term memory is usually assumed to be up to about 1 minute, whereas the long-term memory can be up to a lifetime.

While acknowledging the 'identity theory' and making a conscious attempt to break away from the traditional laboratory-based approach, Baddeley states that there is 'a need to bear both the laboratory and the world in mind in teaching the psychology of memory'. It is well known that someone with dyslexia is likely to have a poor memory. So to whom is the layman to turn? Which view is going to help him most?

In order to understand the apparent aberrations in the functioning of a dyslexic's memory, one must first understand the way in which a non-dyslexic's memory might be expected to work. For this, the most reliable and easily understood model is the laboratory-based model. This is the one we shall be using, but I suggest that, particularly in the field of music, one should always bear in mind that there are other and wider ways in which the memory functions.

If we were to examine in detail in what way musicians commit a piece of music to memory, I suspect that we would find that no particular method is common to all musicians. Everyone has his own 'tricks of the trade', and even these can vary with the instrument that is being played or the piece of music that is being memorized.

Psychologists occasionally suggest that we have a built-in system of forgetting that prevents us from remembering things which in our heart of hearts we do not want to remember. In some instances, this may be true but in others it clearly is not. One 15-year-old boy was selected to have a private trumpet lesson from a famous trumpeter who was due to visit his school. He had been looking forward immensely to the occasion and had been preparing a piece to play to the great man. When the time came, the boy was nowhere to be found – he had completely forgotten. The poor boy could hardly bear his disappointment when he realized what had happened.

In common parlance, we talk about memory as if it were one thing only – one store into which all our experience goes and from which we ought to be able to retrieve any of those experiences we need or want. If we cannot retrieve what we want, we usually say we have a bad memory.

Baddeley points out that memory is not one system but many. He examines short- and long-term visual and auditory memory and quotes some impressive stories of phenomenal feats of memory, some of which will be known to musicians. He tells the story of Mozart memorizing the whole of the Allegri Miserere on hearing it for the first time. He mentions Toscanini, and Mr Napoleon Bird, who, in 1894, publicly played the piano from memory for 44 hours without repeating a composition.

He also quotes the case of Clive Wearing:

> a very intelligent and highly talented professional musician and broadcaster who in his 40s was afflicted by viral encephalitis, which caused inflammation of and subsequently damage to his brain. He was unconscious for many weeks from an attack that would, up to recently, have been sufficient to kill him. However, drugs for treating encephalitis have improved, and his health recovered, leaving him with substantial brain damage and a very dense amnesia… Amnesia is not an all-or-none condition, and most amnesics can appear to be relatively normal on initial meeting. Not so in the case of Clive, since his amnesia was so dense that he could remember nothing from more than a few minutes before…. One aspect of Clive's skills did, however, appear to be remarkably well preserved, namely his musical ability. His wife describes returning on one occasion to find that the choir that Clive had directed was visiting him, and to observe him conducting them through a complex piece of music, showing all his skills and capacity to spot when someone was making a mistake. Similarly, he could play the piano or harpsichord extremely well, although he did initially encounter one particular problem. Many pieces have a point at which a return sign means that that section has to be played once again before continuing. Initially, Clive ran into difficulties at this point, becoming stuck in an apparently eternal loop. Subsequently, however, he appears to have solved the problem of how to cope with this, although it is far from clear how.[1]

A.D. Baddeley 1990

[1] Extract from Baddeley A. 1990 Human Memory Theory and Practice. Reprinted by permission of Lawrence Erlbaum Associates Ltd., Hove, UK.

Kinaesthetic memory

The performance of a piece of music from memory is dependent not only upon long-term auditory memory, but also upon long-term kinaesthetic memory. The two are inextricably linked. Ideally, we recall the sound, which we hope to hear a split second later, and our fingers reach for the keys that will produce that sound. It is quite possible, however, for a series of kinaesthetic actions to take place prompted not by the ear but by a repetition of previous actions. What has been done before will probably be done again if the circumstances are the same. Habits are formed which can become automatic. It is not unlike turning an electric switch on a pianola and watching the keys play themselves. The ability to set the fingers in motion to operate rapid and complicated sequences, uncontrolled by conscious activity of the brain, is an essential constituent in the performance of a memorized piece of music.

Kinaesthetic memory, so often ignored or neglected in the classroom, is sometimes one of the main strengths of a dyslexic. He may have a poor short-term and long-term visual memory, but provided that his long-term auditory memory for music is not impaired, he may be able to achieve the sort of success quoted at the beginning of this chapter. In fact, it is not unknown for a music teacher to be surprised to discover that a pupil she has been teaching for some time has been diagnosed as dyslexic. She may have been worried that he did not seem to be able to sight-read very well, but in all other respects he may have appeared to be just like any other pupil and possibly musically promising.

The child labelled dyslexic when reading, writing and spelling are at stake may have no difficulty over memorizing at the keyboard. The same child may, in fact, be particularly gifted in this area: the kinaesthetic memory can be powerful. The danger lies in his tendency to memorize mistakes. The dyslexic is often aware that he has to work far harder than everyone else. A mistake that may have begun by being a misreading of the score can quickly become a habit through repetition. The habit becomes lodged in the long-term memory, from which there is no escape. When this happens, it is quite useless to try to do anything about it. The time wasted and the frustration generated are negative and unhelpful. If the student were not dyslexic, the chance of success in changing the mistake would be small if he were relying entirely on his kinaesthetic memory. When the student is dyslexic, the chance is probably nil.

If we are aiming for perfection (and what we are doing is learning to play a piece of music rather than learning to sight-read), it is, therefore, absolutely essential that the pupil learns everything – notes, fingering, phrasing and all marks of expression – correctly right from the start. He should not be allowed, tempting as it may be, to hear the piece once and then go and work it out for himself. Mistakes inevitably creep in, and before they can be corrected, they are already on their way to becoming a habit. The best way is to teach the piece from memory, with particular insistence on the correct fingering, never allowing a glance at the score outside the music room. If he gets stuck during the week, he will simply have to wait until the next lesson. When the whole piece has been covered, he can then be allowed to have the score and a tape-recording for reference, by which time he will probably feel that he does not need to use it anyway! However, it can be handy for the teacher when pointing out bars or progressions that need specific practice and for the pupil as a memory jogger in shaky areas.

With young children and beginners, I help them by showing them where on the keyboard to begin, sometimes by means of a picture in their notebooks. I also put in a reminder of the rhythm, usually in the form of words, if it seems necessary and if they can read. It is just too frustrating for them to arrive at home being completely unable to remember their new piece and have nothing to remind them how to start.

Memorizing the architecture

There have been several cases of dyslexic students who have not been able to learn pieces of music in the way described above. They have found the step-by-step, bottom-up method inhibiting and dispiriting. It has not been for them the sort of musical experience to which they have been able to respond in the way in which their innate musicality has demanded. In these cases a different approach altogether has been needed.

I call this the 'top down' approach, by which the student learns to describe the new piece of music in the same way that Hardy describes Gabriel Oak's dog George:

> 'Gabriel had two dogs. George, the elder, exhibited an ebony-tipped nose, surrounded by a narrow margin of pink flesh, and a coat marked in random splotches approximating in colour to white and slatey grey; but the grey, after years of sun and rain, had been scorched and washed out of the more prominent locks, leaving them of a reddish brown, as if the blue component of the grey had faded, like the indigo from the same kind of colour in Turner's pictures. In substance it had originally been hair, but long contact with sheep seemed to be turning it by degrees into wool of poor quality and staple.'

Hardy says nothing about what breed of dog George was, how tall he stood, how long his tail was and whether it waved or wagged. He starts his description as if he were looking down on a well-loved dog whose face was upturned to meet his gaze. He paints the tip of George's nose with consummate care, as being the most delicate and sensitive feature of the whole animal. He then turns his attention to the well-worn coat surrounding the nose and considers the colours within it and the texture of it until we feel as if we would recognize George anywhere.

Translate this into a description of a piece of music and we have the climax, surrounded by what constitutes the build-up towards it and the release of tension after it; the colour of chords and modulations; the contrasting sections balancing one another; the phrases within the sections all going somewhere; the patterns, the echoes in the silences and the tumbling or the soaring of scale passages. Each feature has its own contribution to make to the form of the whole. Every piece that is worth learning has its own architectural balance, its own peculiar character, its own idiosyncrasies, and can be approached as one might design a building by working on the general structure first, followed by the details, until the whole picture emerges, having been in the imagination from the beginning.

This top-down method of learning has a way of imprinting the piece of music on the memory in an experiential way. The piece is experienced and has an impact as a complete entity before every note is examined and analysed. The same care is needed with detail, but it avoids the endless repetition from the beginning and the meaning of the piece as a whole seems to emerge with greater clarity. The skeleton of the work is slowly fleshed out.

If this method is used, the pupil needs to experience the feeling of the whole sound through the fingers of both hands together. For this reason, I believe that the conventional method of practising a piece of music with hands separately at first is not always best. Where some children are concerned, this is comparable to making two separate recordings in their brains. These recordings should run along harmoniously together but, with the slightest weakness in execution, everything can come unstuck. It is common enough for a non-dyslexic pupil to start his piece, setting the two recordings going, and then find that one hand has outstripped the other, perhaps because of a missed rest or something similar: he grinds to a halt, not knowing what has gone wrong. The chances of this happening are even greater for a dyslexic pupil, who may be relying almost entirely upon his kinaesthetic memory.

There is a valuable place for practice with hands separately, but it may be worth reconsidering where that place is in the light of what is known about each dyslexic pupil. Some children may need to learn some passages in their pieces as a complete auditory/tactile experience, possibly stopping every now and again to improve the execution in each hand separately, but making constant reference to how it is going to sound and feel with both hands together.

Opinions differ on the speed for practice that one should advocate to any student. The old dicta 'Slow practice makes slow performance' and 'if you can't play it slowly, you can't play it fast' are still at variance in the music teaching world. For a dyslexic pupil with a short-term memory deficit, it may be very difficult to practise slowly. He may find that he cannot contain the whole phrase in his mind at one time; he may need to practise very short passages up to speed.

It is also hard to hold the whole picture of a piece of music in the mind if slow, separate hand practice is required. For those who prefer to learn the bottom-up method – starting with the detail and gradually working through from beginning to end – the whole picture only begins to emerge when the piece is three-quarters learnt. The top-down method – starting with the shape of the whole piece and gradually delving deeper and deeper into the detail – ensures that the musical experience that the piece has to offer is foremost in the mind of the pupil throughout the learning process. There are potential dangers either way: the loss of form or the loss of detail.

The method chosen will ultimately depend on the way the pupil likes to learn and the way in which the teacher and the pupil work together best. The really musical pupil who can enjoy modulations and cadences will be able to use such landmarks as these to assist his memorizing, or he may have a completely differ-ent, experience-related, personal, holistic picture of the piece in his mind, whereas the less musical may simply need to feel the direction in which the notes are going, relying on his kinaesthetic memory to drive him along. He will still need to know where he is in relation to the whole or he may easily feel disorientated, so a judi-cious mix of both top-down and bottom-up methods may work best in the end.

Whichever method is chosen, the tape-recorder can be invaluable in the early stages. Recordings can be made by the teacher of the whole piece and also of short sections of the piece. The score will only be used for checking fingering. It is not unrealistic to suggest that a dyslexic pupil learns this way: for some, it may be the only way in which they can learn. What is unrealistic is to expect a dyslexic with short-term auditory memory deficit to remember from one week to the next how a piece of music should go.

Sight-reading

Sight-reading – how this word spells doom to so many students! There are plenty of excellent books of pieces for sight-reading, and a bad sight-reader with masses of determination will improve if he practises reading from them every day as much as he can, but he needs to be particularly well motivated to be able to do enough for a significant improvement.

Many of these books offer practical advice on how to set about the task of read-ing at sight. In theory, this is good; unfortunately, in practice, it seldom works unless the reader is already quite good and has an excellent short-term memory. The bad reader forgets almost everything he has painstakingly worked out in preparation. For the examinee on any instrument it is, however, a necessary skill.

It is also the key to the store of wonderful music that has been written over centuries past up to the present day. No teacher can teach even a tenth of the material available that is within the capabilities of her pupil in the time allotted for lessons. If he is going to continue to enjoy playing his instrument after his lessons have stopped, he must try to learn to sight-read.

Let us begin by analysing the problems, some of which will be applicable to every student and some of which are particularly applicable to the dyslexic.

1.   choosing a sensible pulse beat and maintaining it;
2.   remembering the key signature;
3.   forming an aural picture;
4.   reading notes and rests in two clefs;
5.   combining rhythm and notes;
6.   tracking steadily across the page while feeling the way on the keyboard;
7.   looking ahead, remembering what has gone before;
8.   recognizing patterns and intervals;
9.   observing marks of expression;
10. understanding the harmony.

Now let us consider these difficulties one at a time with the dyslexic specifically in mind.

1. Choosing a sensible pulse beat and maintaining it

This, as we all know, is vital to any attempt at sight-reading. The dyslexic is not necessarily going to be any worse at choosing a maintainable pulse beat than is a non-dyslexic, except that he is more likely to panic when he sees an unrehearsed page of notes. This inevitably results in starting too fast, even if the speed he has chosen is actually painfully slow for the character of the music.

How can we help? First, by separating the pulse beat and the rhythm from the sound. This will involve tapping the rhythm of each hand, if necessary separately as well as together, while following the music with the eyes. He will soon find that he has started too fast! Whatever the speed indication at the beginning of the piece, and however easy the first bar, he will have to learn to take it very slowly indeed.

How slowly is slowly? Insofar as one can answer that 'How long is a piece of string?' question at all, one can suggest that the passage should be tapped out at a speed that will allow for the shortest note to be comfortably contained within the phrase. This may mean that the pulse beat is sufficiently spaced to be able, in practice, to walk around the room saying something such as 'This is the house that Jack built' to every step, which will represent the pulse beat. Shorter sentences can be used for faster speeds.

As has been suggested before (Chapter 3), the beat has to be internalized or no consistency in maintaining it will be possible. If there is not space enough in the music room to walk around, the pupil, seated on the piano stool, can sway slowly from side to side. First, he should say whatever sentence has been chosen either by himself or his teacher aloud as he sways, then he should say it silently to himself. Next, having established the speed, he changes to the word 'semiquaver' or 'quaver' or the equivalent in French time names (tafa-téfé or ta-té), according to the length of the shortest note in the piece. Finally, he should notice on which notes in the piece he should be able to repeat the whole of the sentence he used at the very beginning.

Some teachers insist that their pupils count the beats of the bar while sight-reading. Laudable as this is, it will simply not be possible for a dyslexic. Any extra activity beyond trying to sort out the notes will only add extra stress. I have also heard it said, '"And" is the time for looking ahead'. This advice may work for some pupils, but I doubt if it ever works for a dyslexic. His mind will be seething with activity – probably far too much activity – so giving him 'ands' to count between beats will only make things worse.

Even the older and more experienced dyslexic will have to follow through a similar discipline of internalizing the beat before he begins to sight-read.

2. Remembering the key signature

This is where the memory has a part to play – right at the beginning. Ideally, when a pupil sees that there are two sharps in the key signature, he should be able to say to himself, 'This piece is in D major or B minor', and then, having decided between the two keys, he should be able to think in that key and relate everything to it. What usually happens in practice is that the pupil sees the two sharps, says to himself, 'I must remember to play F sharp and C sharp', and then proceeds to play while still basically thinking in C major. If some key sense has been established from the very early stages he then has far less to remember: the F sharp and the C sharp will be implicit in the key of D major (or B minor). Key sense takes a long time to establish but, because it effectively lightens the load on the short-term memory, it is time well spent.

If the dyslexic pupil sees a scattering of sharps or flats in the key signature, it will be important for him, if he has not reached the stage of being able to think in a key, to rehearse each of those notes in his mind so that he does not suddenly switch from sharps to flats or vice versa. He should play the white note and then adjust it to what is required, noticing the relationship between the two.

As when teaching anything, it is so important to be positive. I once came across a piece of sight-reading that had written above it by somebody's teacher 'F major – **no F sharps!**' One can picture the scene only too easily, and I have much sympathy with that teacher, but would it not have been much more effective to write, 'White notes except for B flat'? The dyslexic – not happy with words anyway – might respond even better to a picture of the keys in use.

The layout of the black notes actually assists the memory. One sharp, F♯, is the *lowest* of the bigger group, or trio, of black notes. This is followed by C♯, the lowest of the small group, or pair. The third sharp, G♯, is next door to F♯, so if you have G♯ in the key signature, you automatically have F♯ and C♯ as well. When D♯ is added, you have the next door note to C♯, so there is only one black note that you do not play. By the time a pupil is sight-reading in F♯ or C♯ major, he will undoubtedly have worked out his own method of remembering E♯ and B♯.

Similarly with flats: one flat, B♭, is at the top of the trio of black notes. E♭, the second flat, is at the top of the pair. The third flat, A♭, lies on the middle of the three black notes (as does the third sharp), the next door note to the first black note B♭. D♭ is just below E♭, completing the pair, and G♭ completes the trio of black notes.

Sharps therefore start from the bottom of each group, flats from the top. It may be helpful to establish the order on the keyboard long before the sophistication of writing five sharps or flats in a key signature has been achieved. Then all he has to do is to count the number of sharps or flats in the key signature and follow the pattern on the keyboard.

A little mnemonic may be helpful to remember the difference between sharps and flats: 'Flats fall, sharps shoot.' This will also be helpful for theory (see Chapter 7).

The last sharp or the last flat in the key signature always seems to be the one that escapes notice, yet it is, of course, the most important of them all. With a non-dyslexic, one might suggest to him that he scanned through the piece pinpointing the places where these occurred. With most dyslexics, this idea will probably not work unless he has felt the key under his finger. It is far more effective to suggest that he plays the scale and also the arpeggio before beginning, or even rehearses one octave of the Hanon exercise in the appropriate key (see p.75). This goes some of the way towards helping him to establish that sense of key which he so badly needs.

3. Forming an aural picture

Even if the pupil has had some formal aural training, in the way of solfege or progressive interval work, forming an aural picture of what he is about to attempt to play will be difficult for the inexperienced. The dyslexic may find it almost impossible. Quite often, his aural imagination does not seem to be linked in any way to his visual perception. It is likely that the intervals between the notes on the page will mean nothing to him aurally until he has heard them.

The experienced sight-reader will scan quickly through a piece of sight-reading and will form a fairly accurate aural picture of what the whole piece sounds like. We cannot expect this of the dyslexic pupil. It may be the cowardly way out, but I suggest that the time is much better spent on other things.

4. Reading notes and rests in two clefs

There is a double difficulty here. First, the eye has to take in two staves at once. The distance between the staves can vary according to the printer, the number of systems to be fitted onto one page, the character of the music or the number of marks of expression that the composer has included. In some books, there will be a grossly exaggerated gap, but in others a small gap may be overfilled with instructions of various kinds. Whatever the case, somehow the eye has to be trained to catch both staves in at one glance.

There is, I believe, only one answer to this problem, and that is to write short exercises – not more than four bars – in a jumbo print-size manuscript book with this specific purpose in mind. Plenty of rests should be included. The pupil should tap them out with one hand on each knee. It is not actually necessary to play them all, as long as he taps out several every day (see for example, Figures 6.1 to 6.3).

Figure 6.1

Figure 6.2

Figure 6.3

Practice in reading both clefs together should begin at the Grade 1 stage. There is no need to count as well: this is not what the exercise is for – it is an exercise in visual agility. If, however, he encounters a bar in which both hands rest on the same beat and he fails to recognize this, he should look again at that bar and highlight each beat right through both staves with different coloured highlighters for each beat. He may enjoy doing this right from the start of his training, so it is a good plan to have several photocopies of every exercise handy.

Having several photocopies also allows for the possibility of cutting horizontally between the staves and pasting them either more closely together, so that they relate more intimately to one another, or further apart as the pupil improves. He will need the distance extended as he prepares for a proper sight-reading book.

The second difficulty with reading notes and rests in two clefs is that the notes on the bass stave do not correspond alphabetically to the notes on the treble stave. Trying to read the notes on the page in alphabetical terms and then translate them into places on the keyboard is a laborious process. It is fraught with difficulty for the dyslexic who, using mnemonics in the early stages, may be able to work out what the letter name of the note is, but will then have to choose at what octave he should play that note. It is important (1) to know the names of the notes and (2) to be able to find them on the keyboard, but, for the sake of *sight-reading*, is (1) really necessary?

I have found that the quickest way to understand the geography of the keyboard in relation to the notes on the page is to pinpoint one note only in the treble and one in the bass: the B and the D that fall on the middle lines of each stave. It does not matter what they are called as long as they can be found easily.

The pupil should sit centrally at the keyboard with his hands dangling at his sides. Next, he places his hands on the keys in a direct forward line from the dangling position. They will automatically land on or very near to the B and D of the correct pitch. From these two keys, all the other notes on the stave can be found simply by placing either the thumb or the fifth finger on that middle line key.

It was an 11-year-old dyslexic boy who decided for me how to remember where these keys are. D in the bass is Daddy sitting in the armchair – the pair of black notes being the arms – and B in the treble is for Baby who has fallen off the sofa – the three black notes. This gave him a point of reference so that he could always work out exactly where to start without getting muddled about what any of the notes were called. This pupil's eye function was not impaired in any way except that he could not readjust easily if he had to look from one place to another, for instance from blackboard to exercise book or from music to keyboard. So, having found where to start, he worked everything out by interval and feel, always relating, where possible, to these middle lines.

5. Combining rhythm and notes

This problem can be seen as an extension of the previous one in that the difficulty lies in being able to recognize where each new beat begins and ends, right through both staves. It also involves the skills necessary for choosing a sensible pulse beat and maintaining it.

The visual image has to be translated into a kinaesthetic experience. Add to that the necessity of finding different places on the keyboard for each note, and it will readily be understood that the dyslexic will not have at his disposal the necessary coordination between his faculties to be able to cope.

How can we make it easier for him? This, I believe, is where those flashcards (Chapter 5) again come in. The dyslexic has to have an automatic rhythmic reaction to the sight of different rhythmic symbols. They have to be learnt and practised as often as the words 'the', 'and', 'of', etc. are met with in written language until they are instantly recognized and do not cause a problem.

There are three basic steps in this flashcard exercise:

1.   clapping the rhythm, which has already been discussed (Chapter 5);
2.   tapping the rhythm with one hand while tapping the pulse beat with the other;
3.   alternating the hands so that both become equally familiar with either task.

When these exercises can be successfully accomplished by the pupil, the sound element can be introduced, but as a first step it may be a good idea to represent the *pulse beat only* as a pitched sound. For instance, the pupil plays a note on every beat with one hand while tapping the rhythm on his knee with the other hand. It is important to master each basic step before attempting the next: it is only too easy to come to grief by attempting more than one step at a time unless one is very careful.

6. Tracking steadily across the page while feeling the way on the keyboard

We have already examined the difficulty that a dyslexic has with tracking (Chapter 4).

It may be a considerable effort for him to track through a piece of music from beginning to end even when he is not actually playing it himself. However, he will gain useful experience in the attempt and, as the teacher of reading sometimes practises paired reading with her dyslexic pupils – both teacher and pupil reading along together – so can paired sight-reading, the pupil only reading but not actually playing, help a dyslexic to feel more familiar with the piece as a whole, while at the same time giving him valuable practice in tracking skills.

In order to encourage him to concentrate on the written notes, instead of simply 'switching off' while his teacher does the work, he can be warned that at any moment the music may stop. He will have to point to the place on the score where it has stopped. It can be treated as a game, rather like musical chairs. If he can keep his place he scores a point at every halt, but if he loses his place the teacher scores. This game has the advantage of allowing the more inept pupil to catch up and start afresh at each stopping place. As he improves, so the distance between stopping places can be increased. Eventually, he should be able to track right through.

Tracking being a skill which, on its own, may need concentration, it is important that the pupil is not distracted by looking down at the keyboard. The non-dyslexic can occasionally allow his eyes to flick down momentarily to guide his hands, but it is essential that the dyslexic with tracking difficulties keeps his eyes firmly on the page in front of him.

As with so many other skills, this should be encouraged from day one. The exercises that have been written for him to assist him to read treble and bass clef together can be attempted on the keyboard while the teacher masks his hands from his sight. If the exercise is no longer than four bars and does not involve any movement around the keyboard, there is every chance that he will succeed.

7. Looking ahead, remembering what has gone before

This is another skill that relies heavily on the short term memory, but we need to delve a little deeper into the function of the eyes in relation to the memory in order to understand better what the problem is.

Many researchers (e.g. Mackworth, 1972; Stanley and Hall, 1973; Vellutino et al., 1975) have examined the process of reading in some detail. They suggest that, in order to read a single word, we notice first the way it looks, then how it sounds, then what it means and finally how it is said. These processes can be broken down further, and as an example of how it is done, we shall look at some specific stages that have been suggested.

The argument is that when the eye first lights on a word – when it is presented with a visual stimulus – a snapshot of the visual stimulus is made. This snapshot fades extremely quickly, in a matter of milliseconds, but not too quickly for recognition to take place and to be matched to a memory trace, just as if a photograph of one's mother were momentarily flashed on a screen, one would recognize it instantly because one has a memory of one's mother. This memory trace leads to what is known as an iconic image, which may last for a second or two, as if one saw one's mother in the imagination. While the iconic image is present, it may be said to be in the iconic store.

From the iconic store the word, as we articulate it, moves into the short-term memory, where it may stay for several seconds. The meaning of words and sentences are stored in the long-term memory. When understanding of the word takes place it moves into the long-term memory. If understanding has not taken place, the word will be superceded by the next stimulus and lost altogether.

Further to this sequence of events, when we recognize and understand the word, we may then form an expectation of what is to come next, which may influence the movements our eyes make across the page. Attempts have been made (Eriksen and Collins, 1968; Stanley and Hall, 1973) to measure the duration of the time that visual images remain in their various stores before moving onto the next stage, and it is argued by some researchers (Stanley and Hall, 1973 Badcock and Lovegrove, 1981) that dyslexics differ significantly from non-dyslexics. They suggest that the visual image captured by a dyslexic takes longer to complete the sequence from visual stimulus to being stored in the long-term memory; therefore the risk of being superseded by the next visual stimulus is higher.

Now let us see how this theory may affect the sight-reader of music.

The non-dyslexic sight-reader sees G♯. Because he has seen a G♯ before, he recognizes it as G♯ and he can hold that picture in his mind while he feels for the key and transfers it to his long-term memory by depressing the key that then produces the sound. All is well, and he moves with confidence to the next sound, which contextual evidence may have led him to expect is likely to be an A.

The dyslexic sight-reader, on the other hand may take longer to recognize the note as a G♯. When he has recognized it as being an image that he has seen before, he may be able to hold the picture of it in his mind for longer than a non-dyslexic while he finds the key, but, while he is translating what he sees into movement of the fingers, the next note to be played presents another visual stimulus and the original visual stimulus presented by the G♯ is lost altogether. His eyes will return to the G♯ and, unless and until he has played that G♯, he will be unable to look ahead to the next note.

I believe that the circumstantial evidence for this sequence of events taking place among dyslexics trying to sight-read is overwhelming. There are many other theories for failure in language-based reading among dyslexics, and as every dyslexic is different, one must respect the findings of the researchers. Sight-reading in music, however, bypasses the phonological processes involved in reading language and replaces them with a kinaesthetic process. One would therefore assume that the reason for the inability of some dyslexics to sight-read lies either in the visual process involved or somewhere between the visual process and the kinaesthetic response.

How then can we help? It would seem that what we have to do is to try to speed up the initial processes of recognition and storage, or the iconic store, so that the visual image is realized before it is erased by the next visual image. This means that we have to expose the pupil to a huge amount of visual material so that recognition by matching with an image previously stored in the long-term memory has more chance of success.

The trouble with teaching a dyslexic to play a musical instrument is that one tends to encourage him to play from memory or by ear because that is where he excels. One hopes to encourage him by teaching to his strengths. This unfortunately militates against supplying him with enough visual material to assist his sight-reading. Somewhere a balance has to be struck.

I have heard it suggested many times that if the teacher covers the notes that are being played by her pupil, he will be forced to rely on his memory in order to play them, while his eyes proceed to take in what is to come. This looking ahead is what a good sight-reader does. Every now and again stories are told of phenomenal feats of memory when a sight-reader has been able to look ahead for as much as half a page of notes. It can be seen from the description above that the practice of covering the notes for a dyslexic simply will not work. It will merely call a halt to his attempt.

What can help though is to cover the notes that he has just played, provided that he is already feeling for the next note. This prevents his eyes from working backwards to something he has already played but gives him the security of being able to check the interval to the next note.

The more complex the sight-reading gets, the more likely it is that the dyslexic will not have encountered the particular patterns of notes and rests before. One cannot hope to cover everything – every position of every chord, every cluster of notes and intervals – but unless one has worked as systematically as possible at the visual impression created by notes and chords and their inversions in all keys and in all orientations, that initial snapshot is unlikely to find its matching memory trace.

We say that there is very little contextual evidence to help us when sight-reading, but what little there is can be practised on its own until it becomes almost automatic. As tasks become more routine, the load on the brain becomes lighter, leaving it free to distribute its energy elsewhere. This is an area in which even the experts admit to being only at the beginning (Gathercole and Baddeley, 1993), but for the musician, there is an interesting example of the possibilities of automation: Franz Liszt was known to suggest to his pupils that they read a book while practising scales. Presumably he could demonstrate.

The perfect cadence is perhaps the best example of musical contextual evidence. Figure 6.4 is taken from a book of sight-reading tests for ABRSM Grade 3. Unless the pupil has had enough experience playing cadences in E minor, he is likely to have all sorts of problems here because not only does he have to decide which note the sharp belongs to, but he also has to work out notes on leger lines in both hands. If he has practised the feel of a perfect cadence, he has only one thing to think about instead of several. Each time he plays a scale in practice, the cadence that belongs to it can be practised as well, once he has reached a certain stage of technical competence.

Figure 6.4
© The Associated Board of the Royal Schools of Music. Reproduced by permission

It is also helpful in assisting recognition if the pupil copies cadences into a manuscript book. As with a sculpture, if you cannot recognize it from the back view, you do not know it well enough. They should be practised in all inversions, with any fingering and at several octave orientations.

8. Recognizing patterns and intervals

There seems to be a minority of dyslexic children who have considerable difficulty in remembering geometric shapes (Goulandris and Snowling, 1991). Part of the problem of investigating this phenomenon lies in trying to discover whether the child sees the shape properly in the first place – his perception of it – or whether it is his memory of it that is at fault.

The sight-reader relies heavily on his memory for shapes and patterns. They may be rhythmic or melodic or both: the shape of a broken chord, the rhythmic pattern of a tune just played, and so on. In Figure 6.5, the same rhythmic pattern appears no less than six times (bars 1, 2, 5, 6, 9 and 10) in the 12 bars. Once this has been noticed, and the rhythm of bar 1 has been understood, there are virtually no rhythmic problems left throughout the piece. The first two bars of the tune itself are also repeated identically twice more, the left-hand merely copying the right-hand one octave lower. It is the experienced sight-reader, scanning quickly through the piece for anything that will assist his performance, who will notice these things.

The dyslexic may find this recognition of rhythmic and melodic shapes exceptionally hard. For him, bar 2 may not look in the least like bar 1 because all the stems are reversed, and it begins with a note in a space instead of on a line. In bars 5 and 6, the left-hand begins at a completely different place on the stave and by the time he has reached bar 9, he may well have forgotten what bar 1 looked like.

One is constantly 'joining up the dots' in one's imagination to form shapes of all kinds, which undergo a sort of metamorphosis as they are translated into sound. The wind player uses the sound of the shape in his head to tell his fingers what to do, the string player is guided by his ear, making sometimes quite a different 'shape' on the fingerboard from the shape of the notes on the page. The piano player, on the other hand, maps out on the keyboard the shape he sees on the page. Spatial aptitude is crucial.

Figure 6.5
© The Associated Board of the Royal Schools of Music Reproduced by permission

Studies of the musical, spatial and verbal abilities of children and students in Finland found that age is a relevant factor (Karma, 1982). Musical aptitude correlated more with verbal ability than with spatial ability in 10-year-olds, but the correlation of musical aptitude with spatial ability in young adults was stronger. Karma found that boys of 10 or under who were verbally talented tended to be musically talented, whereas girls, on average, tended to be relatively more talented musically because their verbal talents had developed more quickly. Karma concluded that after the age of 10, spatial ability becomes a more important factor in musical ability and the boys catch up with the girls. Moreover, he noted that spatially talented boys also begin to show good ability to organize sound.

These findings open up some very interesting lines of thought. Is there a correlation between his findings and the suggestions put forward by Lefroy, Cotterell and others (see p.75) that working on a dyslexic's spatial aptitude improves his literacy? If so, the music teacher who perseveres with a pupil with poor spatial ability may be contributing in no small way to his improvement in literacy.

Be that as it may, if a pupil cannot recognize the notes of a triad separately, ascending or descending, or together as a chord, he will have real difficulty with sight-reading. Are they, however, always as easy to recognize as we with our experience find them? Compare Figure 6.6 with Figure 6.7 or with Figure 6.8, where the rhythm element has crept in to confuse matters. Frequent exposure to the various patterns that the simple triad can make is necessary. The dyslexic may take a long time to recognize the similarity between the patterns if his spatial aptitude is poor and if he has not become accustomed to focusing on shapes rather than on individual notes.

Figure 6.6   **Figure 6.7**   **Figure 6.8**

Similarly, the little cliché in Figure 6.9 looks quite different in, for example, the key of F major, yet the fingering and motor control required are identical and soon become automatic once the cliché has been noticed. The dyslexic pupil's attention needs to be drawn to this little shape in all its different locations on the stave whenever it appears in his pieces, so that when he meets it again he will be able to react appropriately.

Figure 6.9

The same exposure to the shape of intervals is needed. It will probably be noticed by the teacher that her dyslexic pupil finds the larger intervals easier to read than the smaller ones. Most sight-reading practice books begin by introducing 2nds and then 3rds and so on, gradually increasing the interval. Would it not be more helpful for the dyslexic to begin by introducing 5ths, then 4ths, and gradually work down to 3rds and 2nds? Whether one then tackles the 6th or the octave is a matter for personal preference and may depend on the stretch of the child's hand, but whatever happens he should learn to feel his way without attempting to look down. The dyslexic will need constant practice in discerning, playing and also writing all the intervals within the octave, and it is only this familiarity with them that will enable him to find his way around the keyboard while he keeps his eyes on the music.

9. Observing marks of expression

One might think that the dyslexic pupil is going to have quite enough to concentrate on with regard to notes and rhythm without trying to read all the other instructions on the page as he goes along.

The easy way out of the dilemma would be to suggest that for the most part he ignore them, but is this not to act down to him and to give the music less than the respect it deserves? He wants to produce a piece of music, which means that he must try to understand as much as he can about the shape of what he is about to play. The marks of expression may be an integral part of the music, and they are there to help the uninitiated, not to hinder them. Some, for example the ritenuto or pause, can be positively helpful if they are observed, because they provide useful breathing space.

What is important about any piece of music? Surely its character. Children can be trained very early on to decide just what the character of a piece is by simply looking at the page, never mind the notes. Before worrying about these, they should ask themselves 'What kind of a piece is this?'

Quite often the answer lies in the articulation. Long, smooth phrase marks often indicate an unhurried, calm, flowing piece, whereas plenty of staccato dots indicate a faster, more lively piece. The dyslexic will probably have to take everything more slowly than it ought to go, so at least when he sees that it should be lively, he should be encouraged to make sure that the articulation is really bright and bouncy. Alternatively, when the piece is smoothly phrased, it is quite often slow enough to make a conscious effort to feel each key beneath the finger before playing it. There is nothing like silence for unnerving one! The continuous flow of a good legato facilitates a feeling of security.

The next important point to establish is where the climax is. Not every piece has a climax, but if there is one, it can usually be located just by looking for the loudest sounds. For a dyslexic, this will probably entail moving his finger along between the treble and the bass staves from the very beginning to the very end of the piece. When he finds an *mf*, for instance, he should pinpoint it with the index finger of his other hand while he continues to look for any other area that may be louder. If he does not do this, he is likely to forget where the original *mf* was. It is always worth making him say the dynamic markings aloud, especially if his auditory memory is better than his visual memory. Having found where the climax of the piece is, he should rehearse at least one beat both before and after it, so that his ear is alerted to the sound as a backup to his eye, which may fail to recognize the dynamic marking at the crucial moment.

Once the climax has been found and rehearsed, the beginning and end of the piece should be considered and the shape of the whole can be drawn, like a mountain, in the air. Sometimes it will have a long, slow slope towards the summit, sometimes a quick one, sometimes it will jump from plateau to plateau and finish triumphantly on the top, sometimes it will finish in the quiet shadows at the bottom. Somehow it must live for the pupil; useful experience can be gained just by looking at the page and talking about the shape and style of the piece. Pupils should be encouraged to form their own ideas on how best to describe the piece.

Expression marks, after all, are a great deal easier to read than notes. The piece can quite often be enjoyed as an entity before a note has been played, and I suggest that carefully chosen sight-reading pieces should be used just for the purpose of trying to build a mind-picture. When the picture has been created, is there any necessity for the pupil to struggle with the notes? Would not the purpose of the exercise – to extract as much information from the page as possible about the shape and character of the piece – be better demonstrated by the teacher then performing it, while the pupil follows the music carefully through, preferably using his own copy?

We have to be realistic. The ability to sight-read is valued highly in the Western world today, but it has not always been so. In countries where the Suzuki method of instruction predominates, sight-reading is only of secondary importance. Time is short. We have to decide how much of it we can spend on sight-reading and how best we can motivate our pupils to practise it. If each preparatory activity were rehearsed properly every time a piece of sight-reading was presented, there would be no time for anything else.

We can halve not only the stress involved in reading at sight but also the time that the activity takes if we divide it into two parts. One day, the pupil can use the time to decide on the character and shape of the piece, possibly even drawing an imaginary picture of it. The next day, he can work on the actual notes.

Sometimes one can play the 'deliberate mistake' game by asking him to identify places where one has 'got it wrong'. A crescendo can be played as a diminuendo or a rallentando as an accelerando and so on. This identification practice is a skill that has now invaded some aural tests in examinations (ABRSM). It is, indeed, part of general musicianship.

10. Understanding the harmony

Having at least some understanding of what the basic principles of harmony are is very helpful for anybody who is attempting to read a piece of music at sight.

When we read the written word, we have contextual clues that play a significant part in the activity of reading to help us. For example, it would be unlikely for anybody to mistake an e for an a and read, 'At nine o'clock he went to bad.' We expect the word 'bed', so that is what we read without working out the vowel sound. In music, it could be argued that there are no contextual clues, but the experienced sight-reader with some harmonic sense will be using contextual clues all over the place to assist in finding the notes. He still has to be on the look-out for the whim of the composer, but often huge chunks of music can be read at a single glance if the player has an ear and an eye for the harmony.

Perhaps the most useful trick of the trade is to be able to play a perfect cadence. These are fun to do and are fairly easily taught. By placing the fifth fingers on the two Cs, two octaves apart, the dominant in the left hand and the leading-note in the right hand can be located and the bare bones of the perfect cadence are already there (Figure 6.10). The semitone between the leading note and the tonic should be noted – in this case two white notes because there is no black note to intervene. A perfect cadence in F major is the next step.

How one proceeds from there is a matter for personal preference. The teacher has to judge according to her knowledge of her pupil's capabilities, but I usually find that children like to learn the skeletons of perfect cadences in all the white note keys before learning to flesh the easier ones out a bit, the idea of the black leading-note being crucial to the keys of A, B, D, E and G.

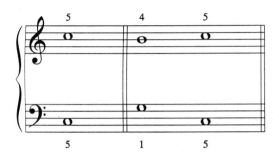

Figure 6.10

But B for Beware! If the perfect cadence in B major is learnt before the scale or the arpeggio, the F♯ for the thumb of the left hand may come as a surprise. It will feel different from the other keys.

Once these skeleton cadences can be played easily, the pupil can either proceed to learn the other five keys (D♭, E♭, G♭, A♭, B♭), which offers the possibility of the sort of progression shown in Figure 6.11, or he can add the right-hand thumb to fill out the chords, as in Figure 6.12. Either way, the contrary motion progression should be noted.

As the learning of these cadences is essentially to assist in sight-reading, it is, of course, only directly helpful if what they look like on the score is learnt at the same time. Long before all the keys are known, the cadences can be written in manuscript, using sharps for the leading notes where necessary.

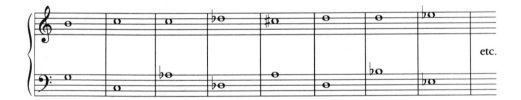

Figure 6.11

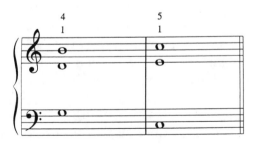

Figure 6.12

C major is not only easy to find on the keyboard, but it is even easier to locate on the stave, both Cs being in spaces, the bass C one up from the bottom space and the treble C one down from the top.

Having learnt both to recognize and to play perfect cadences with the left hand falling from the dominant down to the tonic, the pupil then needs to be able to play and recognize in the score where the bass dominant rises to the tonic. The fourth finger of the left hand plays the dominant, and the thumb then plays the tonic an octave below the treble tonic.

These simple skeletons hold good for both major and minor keys. A knowledge of the dominant–tonic progression is also good aural training and one of the requirements for theory examinations at and above Grade 5 ABRSM. The actual words 'dominant–tonic' should be introduced right from the start, which will make learning all the other technical names a great deal easier when the time comes for them to be known.

Playing duets

In pieces that have been written for sight-reading purposes only, there are fewer contextual clues than in what we might call 'real' music, but one of the real delights for any beginner pianist and more particularly for the dyslexic, who may take a long time to feel that he is making real music, is the playing of duets. There are many examples of famous tunes that have been arranged in duet form. The pupil will get great enjoyment from these, and his ear, knowing what to expect, will eventually help to guide his fingers both rhythmically and melodically. The pupil's part of those that are too complicated in their published form can be arranged in a more simple style. This may not be considered to be true sight-reading, but it is a wonderful way to learn to relate the look of the notes on the page to the feel of the keys beneath the fingers and the sound that completes the picture.

The playing of duets has so much to recommend it that it is almost worth making it an essential constituent of every lesson. The dyslexic whose progress is often slow and laborious can take delight in the sharing of beautiful tunes and rich harmonies, even if his own part is written in octave semibreves. He feels that he is not on his own. He will learn to respond to crescendi and diminuendi, he will be encouraged to feel the swing of the music, and it will give an added richness to his life that I believe is not obtainable any other way. This is the satisfaction that the performer on any other instrument gets when the piano acompaniment is added and which is often the spur that keeps him going.

Summary

This chapter has been about the memory. We have seen how the field of memory is one which still has plenty of room for further exploration. On the other hand, we have seen that the laboratory view of memory to date can help us better to understand how to commit a piece of music to memory. Attention has focused on the advantages and the pitfalls of the kinetic memory and alternative ways of teaching a piece of music to a dyslexic pupil.

From the long-term memory, we moved to the short-term memory skills required for reading music at sight and to the identification of the problems involved in sight-reading. These were listed under 10 different headings, although all of them are closely related to each other. Some of the problems, and perhaps the solutions suggested, are common to all sight-readers, but there are a few that may be of particular significance to the dyslexic pupil. Reading two different clefs bracketed together, combining rhythm and notes, tracking across the page, looking ahead while remembering what has gone before and recognizing patterns and intervals may all be stumbling blocks for dyslexics.

In order to minimize the difficulties, it is recommended that helping the child to internalize as many activities as possible should begin as early as possible. The pulse beat and rhythmic reactions to visual stimuli are two of these activities, but familiarity with the dominant–tonic progression can also be helpful, as can ready recognition of the triad.

Because letters are a problem for a pupil with language-based difficulties, it is suggested that letter names can be left out of the equation altogether and that making an issue of them should be avoided. Provided that he can relate the note on the page to the key on the keyboard, all should be well. Sharps and flats in key signatures can also be correlated directly with the keyboard, bypassing the need for identifying them by letter name.

The spatial aptitude required for sight-reading has been considered, along with the hopeful findings (Karma, 1982) that spatial aptitude, particularly in boys, tends to develop more rapidly after the age of 10. This may be part of the answer to why so many boys find reading at sight so very difficult and why they sometimes overcome their difficulties later on. Indeed, it may be wasted time to worry unduly about sight-reading if a child has marked difficulties in his early years. There are many sight-reading-related skills that can be practised while one waits for those spatial skill developing years. These skills will come into their own at a later stage, and much stress will meantime have been avoided.

Finally, it is recommended that there are several activities which can enhance the learning of sight-reading skills and which may also stimulate general musicianship, besides having a possible knock-on effect in the classroom. Sight-reading should be seen as a way of enjoying music-making, particularly through duets, which can give the pupil intense pleasure. He will experience a sense of achievement in sharing in something of considerably more significance than anything that he could produce on his own.

Chapter 7
Musical theory – coping with writing music

It is quite possible for a music student to become reasonably proficient on his instrument without ever having really understood how what he is playing is represented on paper. This happens many times: the intricacies of note and rest values, along with key relationships, can be overlooked once the melody has been heard frequently enough to have been memorized. If, instead of playing the sounds, the student were asked to reproduce on paper the music he had been learning, he might well founder badly. If he is ever going to be able to work things out on his own, it is necessary for him to understand the mechanics of composition.

Hand in hand with the knowledge of these mechanics is a knowledge of general musicianship. This is a wider and arguably more intuitive understanding of how music is put together. It encompasses elementary harmony, transposition, improvisation and an ability to read a line of melody at sight.

The dyslexic musician may have strengths in the field of musical composition, but it can be frustrating for him to have a tune in his head or at his fingertips that he is not capable of writing down in order that other people may play it. The many hours that musicians in the 'pop' world spend in playing together and conveying music by ear to one another could be halved – at the very least – if the members of the group were all musically literate as are members of a conventional orchestra. The 'pop' musician who can write music is much in demand.

This chapter addresses the problems that a dyslexic may have in relation to learning to write music, or in surmounting the barriers in the form of obligatory examinations, in what is loosely termed the theory of music, to progressing further than Grade 5 ABRSM practical examination. The term 'theory' will be used in the narrow sense of the mechanics of written music.

More and more books for beginners are being written which integrate the learning of theory with its practical application. They often have cheerful and colourful illustrations as well as puzzles and games. Unfortunately, there are seldom enough illustrations of the same point to make a reasonable impression on a dyslexic. He will almost certainly have to have many exercises tailor-made for him alone.

Also included in this chapter are some ideas about the best use of the note-book, which many teachers give to their pupils as an *aide-mémoire* for practising.

Materials for writing music

As spoken language precedes written language, so articulated music precedes written music. For several years before formal music lessons are undertaken, the child has probably been exposed to all sorts of musical songs both at home and in nursery school. As with written language, so we need to begin his musical education in the theory of music from the age at which he can first manipulate a pencil.

This competence with a pencil is where the dyslexic is at a disadvantage. The fine motor skills required for the accurate representation of music may be difficult for him to acquire. All the more important for him to begin early and to practise regularly. There is a spin-off in the classroom if the dyslexic has learnt something of the high standard of precision that is required for transcribing music. It is occa-sionally suggested that good handwriting is not really of much importance now that communication relies on the telephone, the word-processor and the computer. There are computer-based music systems in existence that perhaps one day will be so commonplace that neat writing on the stave becomes an obsoles-cence, but that day is still in the future. Before one can begin to teach how written music fits together, one has to address the problem of neatness.

Neat, comfortable writing is best achieved if the pupil has a relaxed and natural grip on his pencil. It is commonplace for dyslexics to have a cramped grip that militates against freedom and control of movement. The controlling fingers should be sufficiently far away from the point of the pencil to allow him to see clearly exactly what he is doing. Pencil grips can be bought commercially that encourage the correct positioning of the fingers.

It is worth giving some consideration to the choice of materials one uses for the theory lesson. The dyslexic may slightly resent having to use pencil and paper at all during a music lesson, so it is common sense to make the experience as pleasur-able as possible. The physical sensations should be relaxed and enjoyable. Use good-quality paper, well-sharpened pencils with neither too hard nor too soft and woolly a lead – a B or an HB is good – and an extremely effective eraser!

The right-handed pupil has the advantage of being able to write with an over-head projector pen on manuscript paper that has been inserted into a plastic sleeve without making a mess (see Chapter 4). Jumbo-sized manuscript paper is necessary for this. Whether the pupil is left- or right-handed, the best size of manuscript paper should be found for him: large enough to be able to see clearly but small enough for him to be able to fill in crotchet heads quickly.

Music is invariably written black on white. The dyslexic may feel much more comfortable using colour. Until erasable colour pencils are available, it will be necessary to stick to an ordinary lead pencil, but there is no reason why manu-script paper should not be photographed on to a coloured sheet, provided that it has a good surface. Experimenting with different materials is well worth the time and trouble if what suits him best is eventually found.

In many theory books, the spacing has to be copied from a model, in which case the notes to be written should be copied precisely below the model. Copying requires adjusting the focus of the eyes from the model to the replication. The adjustment is only small if the answer to the question is on the same piece of paper as the model. If work is being done from the blackboard, as it is occasionally in schools where music theory is taught in class, the adjustment required is much greater and can cause real distress for a dyslexic. Not only does he have to make the adjustment of focus, but he also has to convert the angle of perception from the vertical blackboard to the flat page on the desk. Moreover, he has to hold in his memory each representation as he makes this adjustment. It will be readily appreciated that, for a dyslexic, theory is much better learnt away from the blackboard.

The reproduction of musical symbols

Let us begin with the treble clef. This is a beautiful shape, but it is so full of curvacious lines going this way and that that anyone with fine motor and/or spatial aptitude problems invariably has difficulty in drawing it.

There are two schools of thought about which end of the line to begin: at the bottom with the hook or at the centre with the spiral. Neither is ideal for the child who is being taught in the classroom to begin his letters at the top, which is a general rule for most styles of cursive writing, but, if he has not already developed the habit of starting letters from the bottom, then starting drawing the treble clef at the centre of the spiral is much the better. It ensures the correct placing on the stave and reinforces the principle of top-to-bottom in the sweep of the final vertical line.

Besides the well-known way of teaching the shape of the treble clef by converting a solid line into a dotted line that the pupil then joins up, there are other ways that can be used to help him to gain a more indelible impression of what the shape is and how he can reproduce it. Ask him to draw it in the air, guiding his arm for him if need be, or allow him to roll out a plasticine snake and turn it into the clef shape. In the classroom, a sand tray might be used for patterning letter shapes. This teaching aid is not readily available in the music room, but a small tray with a handful or two of rice or split lentils sprinkled over it works almost as well and feels nice. It is also cleaner! Whatever method is used, the child must always start the shape in the same place and use one unbroken line.

The bass clef is far easier. Until recently music publishers were at variance as to which way round it should go, but it now seems to be universally printed 𝄢. If the two dots used to identify F are taught first as lines, as in an F, it helps to draw attention to the fact that the placing of the dots is important.

The symbol for any kind of note should always begin with the note head, and the stems always added starting at the top. Dyslexics who are having trouble with the orientation of bs, and ds, and ps and qs, may have the same trouble with the stems of notes. If the child draws a picture at the top of the page of a *lowered* stem on the *left* of the head and a *raised* on the *right* of the head (see Chapter 4), he can use these pictures for reference while he is working, instead of having to think about it every time he draws a note.

The dyslexic with fine motor problems stemming from a deficit in his spatial aptitude is probably going to have difficulty with spacing the notes out evenly. There are several different ways of helping him with this. The most common is to suggest that he leaves the width of a finger between each note as he would between words. Alternatively, if the space available is too limited for this, he can use the width of a pencil.

It can be a help, particularly for the dyslexic with a good auditory short-term memory, to work aloud. For example, if the pupil is writing out the notes of a scale, he should say aloud 'Line, space, line, space' or 'C, D, E, F', and so on. One cannot guarantee that he will not miss a line or a space – he may be quite capable of drawing a note on a line when he is saying 'space'. – but there is more likeli-hood that he will eventually notice that he has gone wrong if he hears himself describing what he is doing.

Every time a scale has to be written out, the notes should be numbered 1, 2, 3, 4, 5, 6, 7, 8 – being careful to see that 1 is at the bottom and that if 1 is on a line, 8 should be in a space. This ensures that there are the right number of notes in the scale and it also makes identifying any one of them much quicker.

The symbols for rests are easily confused, and the crotchet rest in particular is exceptionally difficult to draw. It is advisable to make crotchet rests completely different from quaver rests, rather than using the reversed quaver rest for a crotchet, because of the difficulty of remembering which orientation to use. The shape should be practised as a wavy line all down the page, first: wave to the right, wave to the left, or wave forwards, wave backwards like a snake. Then add the sting in the tail (or the head!) with the little hook backwards, as in Figure 7.1.

In order to help my pupils to distinguish between the minim and the semibreve rest, I tell them all, whatever their age, the story of the two monkeys who climbed the tree. The little 2-year-old monkey took fright when they reached the third branch and decided to sit tight and go no further. His big 4-year-old brother boldly climbed on to the next branch, but, as he let go of one hand to wave down to his little brother, he slipped. It was only his tail that saved him from falling off

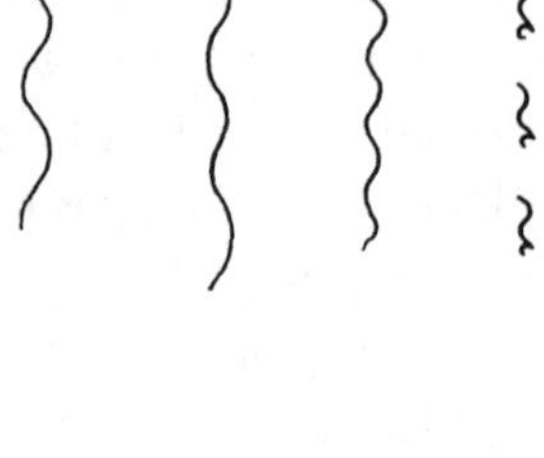

Figure 7.1

altogether. As it was he landed up on the under side of the branch. It may be a babyish story but it works.[1]

Method

Music theory can be divided loosely into four categories:

1. rhythm;
2. pitch (keys);
3. harmony;
4. performance.

Each category has many subdivisions. For example, rhythm can be understood to include all time signatures and the notation for both simple and compound time, the rhythmic notation of words, phrasing and ornaments. It can seem extremely complicated but it is in fact quite logical, and one does not have to be a mathematician to be able to cope with it, although admittedly it might help if one were!

The dyslexic pupil is not one who can gradually assimilate information in an orderly way. Cast him off on a sea of theory and he is going to sink without trace unless he has a few lifelines to the shore. The most important lifeline is method. He should learn a few simple guidelines on how to set about answering questions, which will stand him in good stead whatever he is doing and at whatever stage he happens to be.

Provided he can read, he will first of all have to sort out what the question means and what he is required to do. Questions in examination papers frequently have more than one instruction to be followed. Each instruction is usually, but not always, contained in a separate sentence. Take the following typical example:

> 'Using the given rhythm, write either the harmonic or the melodic minor scale in each of the keys named below. In the brackets, write the name of the form (harmonic or melodic) that you have used. Do not use key signatures: write separate accidentals for notes that need them, and add ⌐‾‾⌐ signs to mark the semitones.'

Anybody has to be fairly clear-minded and methodical to answer this question; the dyslexic is only going to get about half of it answered, if he is lucky, and he will waste much time in going backwards and forwards over the same ground wondering whether he has remembered everything.

The first thing he must do is to count the number of sentences, regardless of their meaning. All too often a dyslexic fails to notice punctuation (see p.56), but if he is only required to find the full stops, without simultaneously trying to read the sentences for meaning, the task immediately becomes much easier. He should ring the full stops in pencil, numbering each one. If there are three full stops, as in the instruction above, he should write 1, 2, and 3 beside each exercise he has to complete.

---

[1] If the terms 'whole note' and 'half note' are used for the semibreve and minim, the story can easily be altered to one about a 1-year-old monkey and his little $1/2$-year-old brother.

The second point he should look for is any instruction given regarding the key signature. If it has to be included, he should either underline the point in pencil or write Y or N, for Yes or No, beside the numbers.

He is now ready to tackle each part of the question separately. As he completes the first part, he cancels out the number 1 and moves to the second part, cancelling out number 2 at its completion, and so on until he has finished. He may decide to do all the number 1s first, then all the number 2s and then the number 3s. It does not particularly matter as long as he ends up with all the numbers cancelled out. He should also cancel out the Y or N when he has checked that he has done what was required. The method above divides the question into manageable chunks and offers a simple plan of campaign. Right from the start and long before examination questions have to be answered, the child should develop an attacking frame of mind, which he can only do if he knows how to begin.

Whenever possible, it is a good idea not to rely on the short-term memory. The trick is to write things down. Let us take a simple example. The pupil is asked to 'Add the missing bar lines in the following, which all start on the first beat of the bar' (Figure 7.2). Let us assume that he knows that the time signature means 3 quavers (or 3 eighth notes) in a bar. He should proceed to write 1+1 over the first crotchet (or quarter note), because it is worth 2 quavers, 1 over the quaver B, 1+1 for the next crotchet and so on. Each pair of semiquavers should be enclosed by a circle and have 1 written above the circles. Having gone right through, he then inserts the bar lines after every third 1 between his pencilled numbers and, if it all seems to fit, transfers the bar lines onto the music.

Figure 7.2
© 1990 The Associated Board of the Royal Schools of Music. Reproduced by permission

This method is another example of how some guidelines can help. If, during the exercise, the pupil is likely to forget that he is dealing with a quaver beat, he should write above his working ♩ = 1, ♪ = ½ or even ♩ = 1+1, whatever suits him best. If he gets into the habit of helping himself by using these little strategies, he will have far less to remember on a short-term basis.

Understanding rhythm

This is a real minefield. We have to use all the imagination and ingenuity we can muster to explain clearly and in a memorable way how the rhythm jigsaw fits together. There are endless little conventions that have to be superimposed on the sheer mathematical problem. How can we make it easier?

As with every other many-faceted subject, let us break it down into those manageable chunks again and see if there is some colourful way of making each chunk come alive.

Any teacher with an apple and a sharp knife handy, can explain about semi-breves, minims, crotchets, quavers and semiquavers. The dyslexic is probably going to have a problem with remembering the rather complicated names and may prefer the American equivalent of whole note, half-note, quarter-note, eighth-note and sixteenth-note. Two half apples being the same value as one whole apple seems to make better sense than two minims being equal to a semi-breve, but he will eventually have to learn the terminology used outside America. The pupil having become accustomed to the values of the notes, is now going to need a great deal of practice in manipulating these basic tools of his trade.

Writing notes and frequently having to rub them out again is seldom fun. Even if the final result is correct and gets a bold red tick or a star, it often looks untidy and unsatisfactory. What is much quicker, involves no rubbing out and introduces the element of a game about it is to have a pack of playing cards with representations on them of all the basic symbols – notes and rests. These can be shuffled about and grouped together in endless different ways. Educational suppliers (see 'Appendix') have packs of blank cards, or one can make one's own, using thick card. Besides the notes and rests, one needs time signatures, bar lines and double bar lines. Unless a very large table is available, it is advisable to make rather small cards.

If time is not too much of a problem, one can play a sort of rummy with these cards, or even pelmanism. The trouble is that time usually is a problem, but this sort of approach often works and in the end is a saving of time.

Until the basic note and rest values are thoroughly known, it is best to steer clear of the beam. Quavers and semiquavers can be written separately or, if one is using cards, represented as separate items. It should be pointed out that all tails on stems go on the right, whichever side of the stem the head is on. It can be helpful to put an arrow pointing to the right before the work is begun, or have a coloured 'post-it' label with a drawing on it to show both ♪ and 𝄾.

When the beam is introduced, it can be helpful to think of it as something more relevant to everyday life than a mere straight line. A collective noun works quite well – birds have two legs (quavers), horses have four legs (semiquavers) and so on.

Keys

As with rhythm, so with pitch: there are *aides-mémoire* that can be written down on a spare piece of paper before tackling any question concerned with keys or note names.

Elementary theory exercise books introduce the whole subject of keys very gradually. They tend to begin with C major and progress slowly through the majors and minors until all the sharps and flats are learnt. This works splendidly, but it is possible to go a very long way without ever having really understood how they all fit together and, in particular, how the majors and their relative minors are interlinked. Nor does the above method provide a point of reference to which the pupil can refer if his mind goes blank. How many flats has E♭ major, or how am I going to remember the key signature for C♯ minor?

The first little reminder is simply the alphabet up to G. The dyslexic pupil may have managed to learn the alphabet, but he may not find it at all easy to say it in reverse. In order to find any relative minor key from its relative major, it is important to be able to calculate the third letter name below the keynote of the major key. If the pupil writes from A to G twice, starting at the bottom of the page with one letter on each line, he will have an immediate handy reference.

Having written the alphabet up the page, the pupil should then circle the A, link the B to the C, circle the D, link the E to the F and circle the G. This should be repeated for the second octave. Circle–link–circle–link–circle. Now he should put a horizontal line above and below each of the circled letters, noticing that the line between G and A does a double job (Figure 7.3).

Figure 7.3 is, in effect, a picture of an up-ended keyboard. It will stand the pupil in good stead whenever he is required to work out relative majors and minors. The heavy horizontal lines show the positioning of the black notes on the keyboard so that, when calculating the three semitones between the major and its relative minor, or the minor and its relative major, each step, or semitone, can be easily seen without having to remember which letter names are only a semitone apart.

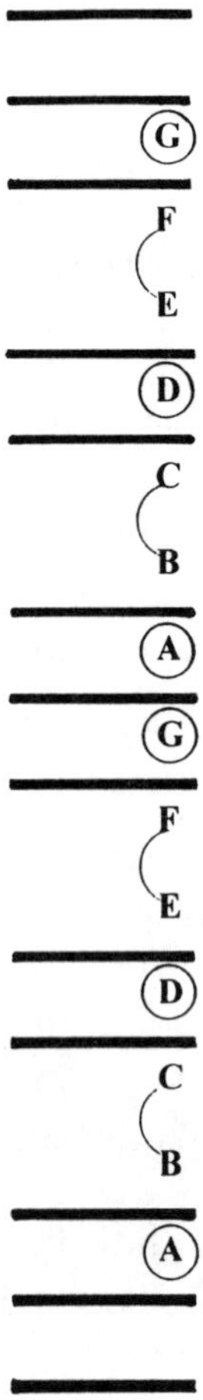

Figure 7.3

He should be thoroughly conversant with finding the names of notes that are the third letter name and the third semitone above or below a given note before attempting to write the notes of the scales or chords of these relative major or minor keys. For example, he may be asked, 'What is the name of the note which is a minor 3rd below B?' He may count down 3 semitones – 'B to B♭ – one, B♭ to A – two, A to A♭ – three' and come up with A as the answer, which is of course wrong. If he has the picture – the pictorial representation of the keyboard – in front of him, and knows that the answer should be something to do with the third letter name as well as the 3rd semitone, he is much more likely to give G♯ as the correct answer.

A problem may crop up here with the concept of above and below. Writing the letters A to G up the page rather than across it goes a long way towards circumventing this problem. Teachers will have their own favourite ways of demonstrating how to remember that the relative minor is to be found below the major. If the vertical alphabet is used, the opportunity for relating a tall man (the major) to a shorter cousin (the minor) presents itself and can be graphically demonstrated, but this is purely a matter for personal choice and imagination. As with so many other points, the best way may be to work out with the pupil what would be most meaningful to *him*. (I have to admit that I cheat over the spelling of minor in this context, although I do explain – more than once – that there are two ways of spelling the word that sounds like 'minor'. I draw a picture of a miner digging for coal under a hill and on top of the hill is the Major in uniform marching along. The purist might consider this anachronistic and unhelpful, but, in order to establish the major/minor principle, it seems to work.)

The most useful reminder, after the alphabet, is, without a doubt, the sentence 'Father Charles Goes Down And Ends Battle'. (Readers will have come across other sentences that give the order of the sharps and flats in key signatures and no doubt they work just as well, but I use this one because it makes sense backwards). This sentence must be learnt from memory – there is no alternative – but if it is instilled in the child as soon as possible, it will eventually save him hours of time and much anxiety. It is far easier remembering one sentence and knowing how to manipulate it than trying to remember the 12 keys and all their key signatures. When he is thoroughly familiar with it, it can be abbreviated to F C G D A E B.

Armed with these two reminders – Father Charles Goes Down And Ends Battle written across the top of the page and the alphabet written up the side of the page – the child has two lifelines to which he can cling whenever a question of key comes up. (It can be useful to add another F [F for Fierce?] in brackets after 'Battle', so that there is an F at both ends of the sentence, for the pupil who cannot remember when reading from right to left for flat keys that F major has a B♭ .)

When there is any difficulty over remembering the difference between ♯s and ♭s and how to find the keynote from a given key signature, I use the little mnemonic 'Sharps Shoot, Flats Fall'. In fact it is sometimes useful to add a 'Fourth' after 'Flats Fall'. The pupil then always calculates the key from the last ♭ or ♯. F♯ shoots up to G (major). B♭ falls a fourth to F (major). If the vertical alphabet is handy, it is only a matter of counting to find the keynote of the major key.

Mnemonics are often recommended as a useful memory aid, but there is no doubt that they can be overused. What is that one for remembering the planets? It must have a V for Venus in it somewhere, and a J for Jupiter . . . . It can be just as difficult to remember the mnemonic as to remember the list it represents. Mnemonics abound for remembering the names of the lines and spaces on the bass and treble clef staves. Even assuming that the dyslexic has committed these to his long-term memory, what happens when he is faced with the C clef? He will have to count lines and spaces. Here again, his vertical alphabet is invaluable. If he is uncertain of the notes on the treble and bass staves, he can even continue the alphabet for a third octave and, putting an 'X' beside the most central C, he can work out where all the lines of the two staves are. In practice, one usually finds that his instrumental work has necessitated the learning of the notes in at least one clef, but often he is unable to relate his instrumental experience to its theoretical application. Constant reminders that the treble and bass clefs are clefs with letter names that indicate specific lines can also be helpful.

Pupils are often asked to distinguish between the harmonic and the melodic minor scale. This is yet another point that can be taught multisensorily: all that is needed is a piece of paper with 13 squares in a row drawn across it, and 13 tiddlywinks. Only 8 tiddlywinks are strictly necessary – one for each degree of the scale – but somehow 13 seems to give more satisfaction. It may not help every pupil; some may prefer only 8. The squares represent the 12 semitones in a scale plus. Number the tiddlywinks 1 through to 8, leaving the remaining ones blank. I use red ones for the tonics at either end and also for the 2nd, 4th and 5th degrees of the scale – the intervals from the tonic which are invariable. Place the numbered tiddlywinks as for the major scale on the appropriate squares on the paper as in Figure 7.4.

Figure 7.4

Now tiddlywinks numbers 3 and 6 can be moved one square to the left or down a semitone, covering the blank tiddlywinks to show the harmonic minor scale. Alternatively the 3rd alone can be moved a semitone to show the ascending melodic minor, and then the descending form can be demonstrated by moving both the 7th and the 6th down a semitone. For those who feel happier with the numbers in ascending order up the page, it is a simple matter to turn the paper so that number 1 is at the bottom.

By actually manipulating the tiddlywinks from one place to another, the dyslexic has a much better chance of understanding the different forms of the scale than if he were merely writing symbols on a page. He can also see the semitones more clearly. Another and even better dimension is added to the exercise if he can sing the sounds as well.

The writing of 4 part harmony begins with the writing of the triad. It is here more than anywhere that untidy writing can often lead to wrong answers. It is useful in the early stages for the pupil to get into the habit of checking that, if the bottom note of a triad in root position is on a line, the top note is also on a line. Tiddlywinks can come into their own again: a large five line stave drawn on a piece of card and four tiddlywinks enhance learning by introducing a more vivid kinaesthetic experience.

After a while, there inevitably comes the confusion between 'root' and tonic', even with non-dyslexics. This can be prevented to some extent if the pupil is encouraged to name the notes of the triad 'root', 'third', 'fifth' when he first begins to write triads. At this stage, it can also be useful for the pupil to put an 'X' beside the root of the chord. This prepares the way for recognizing inversions later on.

In the classroom, the dyslexic is frequently required to 'look–cover–write–check'. The checking in the classroom context refers to comparing what he has copied with the original. There are two things needing checking in music theory which are common to many of the questions on theory that a pupil has to answer. Both begin with the 'k' sound – as in 'check': they are key (signature) and clef. All too often the pupil is so concerned with what he has written down himself that he fails to relate his working to what has perhaps been printed already – the clef and/or the key signature. Having made himself a list of the parts of the question that have to be answered (see above), he must learn to check his working.

Another useful habit for the dyslexic to acquire is the habit of writing down the names of notes. He should get accustomed to checking these with the key signature every time, always on the look-out for the dominant chord in the minor key, because it includes the sharpened 7th of the scale.

Performance indications

Included under this heading are the many signs, Italian terms or other indications on the page that relate to performance. The most common signs – the dot for staccato, the phrase mark and the slur, the dots for repetition and the fermata – are met fairly frequently in the practical music lesson. Ornamentation is largely a rhythmical problem, also frequently encountered in practical performance and related to the interpretation of sound rather than to the application of words. The difficulties that a dyslexic may have over these details of performance may not be very different from those which confront non-dyslexics. Difficulties may arise if he is required to put a name to the smallest note values such as demi-semiquaver or even hemi-demi-semiquaver. In practice, each subdivision of the words means an extra line halving the length of the note. That is the substance of what he needs to know.

The real problem for a dyslexic lies in the translation of Italian terms. There are over 200 Italian terms (not to mention French and German ones) that are in use in musical performance and which should be known. The dyslexic will quail. It is quite probable that his reading of the English language is still at a fairly elementary stage; how is he going to cope with Italian?

It is recognized now that there are three basic phases in the acquisition of reading skills (Frith, 1985):

1. the logographic phase, in which the child guesses the word by its shape;
2. the alphabetic phase, in which he uses his knowledge of the sounds that the letters make;
3. The orthographic phase, in which he uses his knowledge of all the rules and conventions he has learnt.

He also uses contextual clues.

When it comes to an isolated Italian word, there are no contextual clues. Nor has he learnt any spelling rules to help him with pronunciation, which might assist him to form an auditory approximation of the word, which in turn might enable him to make a fair guess at it. He is much more likely to regress to the logographic phase and guess the meaning of the Italian word from the shape of some English word that looks much the same. Hence he may translate 'lacrimoso' as evil, being to do with crime, or 'mosso' as soft – being mossy.

Italian terms are, like so many other things, best learnt in the practical lesson so that they are encountered and revised frequently, but there are a few general rules that can help. These mostly refer to word endings, which can be highlighted by the pupil.

1. -endo or -ando endings are words to do with -ing, the gerund. For example, rallentando = getting slower, diminuendo = getting quieter.
2. -mente indicates an adverb, therefore -ly. For example, largamente means broadly.
3. There is no 'x' in Italian, therefore 'expressive' in English becomes 'espressivo' in Italian – nothing to do with coffee!

Beyond that, it is difficult to generalize.

There will be many words that the serious student will simply have to commit to memory because his powers of informed guesswork will be inadequate. It is for these words that an indexed notebook is invaluable.

First, the Italian word is entered under the appropriate letter. It is best if he writes it himself, trying to learn the spelling as he does so. He should pursue the policy of 'Look–Cover–Write–Check'. Not only should he look at it carefully in the first instance, but he should also say the letter names; his auditory short-term memory may be better than his visual short-term memory. He should try to commit the Italian word to his long-term memory by repeating it many times, 'chunking' it into separate syllables if need be, and frequent revision (overlearning) should be done. It might be pointed out at this stage that the rule for a soft c and g is the same as in English but the c is pronounced ch as in 'cherry'.

Second, the pupil decides what little picture would serve as a clue to remind him what the word means. There are indications throughout the world of education that future generations will become pictorially, rather than linguistically, minded. Computers can scatter meaningful pictures throughout a composition; a heart signifies love, a clock means time and so on. But pictures can have very personal connotations. On one occasion, my pupil tried to think what word for 'legato' would best illustrate 'smooth' for her. She eventually decided on 'Custard'. Somewhat nonplussed, I did a very amateur drawing of a pudding plate full of something yellow, but she has never forgotten what 'legato' means!

The picture clue accompanies the Italian term on the same page. Overleaf is the proper translation, just in case he still cannot remember what the word means or if he needs to check.

It should be remembered that there are no Italian musical terms beginning with h, j, k, w, x, y or z. There is only one q, 'Quasi', and both u and i have very few examples. The notebook therefore is perhaps better made at home than bought commercially.

Practical Musicianship

The examination in Practical Musicianship at Grade 5 is offered by the ABRSM as a qualifying alternative to Grade 5 theory. It may be a more practical option for the dyslexic. If the dyslexic is proficient on his instrument, has a good auditory memory and can improvise, it could well be that he might not find practical musicianship too demanding, although it is not an easy option if he finds reading even one line of music very hard.

There are requirements for practical musicianship examinations that reflect the skills that any musician needs in the course of learning to play an instrument. Even if actually attempting to take the examinations would be an exercise not worth the risk, there is much to be gained, especially for the dyslexic pupil, in studying those skills. There are exercises in the early stages that require just that approach to internalizing rhythm which makes the superimposition of melody more possible. Tapping a simple ostinati rhythm while listening to a tune superimposed upon it helps to train the mind in the first steps of being able to play with hands together at the keyboard. Similarly, spotting mistakes in a one line score is wonderful training for aural awareness allied to visual acuity. It is also a subtle way of practising score reading without the tension that creeps in when notes have to be found on the keyboard. Singing at sight combines rhythm and melody without the added complication of a kinetic element. For a dyslexic with spatial difficulties, this is easier than instrumental sight-reading, and the support from the keyboard accompaniment is helpful.

As the pupil progresses, he will be expected to interpret ornamentation, but this may be easier for him than writing it down. Natural instincts and experience come to the fore, unencumbered by pencil and paper.

The notebook for practice

There are three reasons for making use of a notebook for practice:

1.   as a reminder to the child as to what he has to practise for the following lesson;
2.   as a reminder to the teacher to hear everything he has practised;
3.   as an indication to the child's parents that specific work has been done and must be consolidated. It can also be used to record encouraging progress.

I suspect that, if we were concerned with a non-dyslexic child, I have listed these reasons in the reverse order of their importance to the people concerned. That is to say that it is invaluable for the parents to know what has been done in the lesson and what has to be practised, it is a useful reminder for the teacher if she has failed to make a full assessment of the lesson in her own notebook, and the pupil, if he remembers to look in it at all, will only glance at one or two headings.

This is to be expected when we are dealing with pupils who find words difficult. The notebook should therefore be as attractive as possible to look at, and words should be kept to a minimum. Pictures are more graphic than words, even if they are not particularly good pictures, and colour is always a help.

If something needs practising at least five times every day, it is a good idea to have a little chart drawn out on a 'post-it' label and stuck either in the music book or in the notebook. The pupil can then cross out the appropriate numbers or put a coloured adhesive sticker on each square every time he practises. It is much easier to persuade any child to practise a tricky area if he knows how many times he has to do it. If it is announced that a train is going to be late, one can accept it far more readily if one is told how long one must wait than if one is given no information. Every train that draws into the station one expects to be the right one, and the disappointment gets worse and worse. If you say to a child that he must work at a passage five times, he knows that there will be an end to the exercise, and it gives him an added impetus at each repetition to get it right.

The notebook itself can so easily get lost – what teacher does not know this? – if the child is typically disorganized. It is often worthwhile attaching it to his music book rather than allowing it to sink to the bottom of his music case and become so crumpled that it is impossible to use. It should be something helpful and friendly rather than something that causes stress. 'Post-it' labels can be used, in addition to the notebook, to draw attention in the music book to areas that need particular attention.

Some teachers advocate offering rewards for work well done. This is a practice that can go wrong and lead to disappointment. It would be dishonest to reward an unsatisfactory performance, yet the child may have tried very hard to get it right. Would it not be better to offer a reward for evidence that the child had tried hard, perhaps because he has remembered to fill in his practice chart each time he has practised, rather than to suggest that he gets a reward for a good performance? That reward can come as a surprise, not as the result of what amounts to a bribe, although which one of us has not resorted to bribery at times?!

Most children up to the age of about 11 or 12 love collecting things. Stars can be awarded and stuck in the practice notebook all together on one page if that idea appeals to them. Red stars can be used for scales, yellow for sight-reading and so on. There has to be a 'feel good' factor attached to the notebook.

Summary

The theoretical side of learning about music is one that tends to be neglected in favour of the hands-on experience, but the serious student has to face it sooner or later. There is a great deal to assimilate even at an elementary stage; therefore, the earlier the process begins, the better.

The choice of materials can make a big difference to how much the dyslexic is going to enjoy learning and how much pleasure he takes in the finished result. A multisensory approach encourages him to enjoy and to remember shapes and signs that are peculiar to music alone.

Daunting questions in examination papers need to be tackled in a level-headed manner, beginning by counting the number of sentences. If there are, for instance, three sentences and two different examples to be completed, then 1 2 3 should be written beside each example and each number cancelled out as it is done. Method is invaluable: the pupil should learn to help himself and lighten the load on his memory by writing things down. He must learn to proceed step by step, not attempting more than one thing at a time.

In the initial stages, cards with note and rest symbols drawn on them can be used to accustom the child to note values. Games of ever-increasing complexity can be played, so that eventually he has a thorough understanding of how rhythmic patterns work.

Two particularly useful reminders should be written down at the start of any work involving keys: the F C G D A E B across the top of the page and the alphabet from A to G, at least twice, starting from the bottom of the page. Long before all the keys need to be known, it is invaluable for the pupil to know how the system works. Once he has understood this, and proved to himself that he can manipulate it, it does not matter how complex the question becomes: the method is always going to be the same.

Italian terms should be indexed in a special notebook. The pupil can be encouraged to use his auditory as well as his visual memory to help him to remember spellings. Help can be given with pronunciation, too, in case the sound of the word initiates a memory of the English equivalent.

The study of practical musicianship skills may appeal to the dyslexic more than written theory. This is an area in which his natural gifts may help him to overcome his fear of the score.

In conclusion, we have seen in this chapter that a notebook for recording lessons and listing what the pupil has to practise can be useful not only for the pupil, but also for his parents and for the teacher herself. If the pupil is going to be encouraged to use it properly, it needs to be aesthetically pleasing and to be seen to have some purpose.

Chapter 8
The lesson and the wider world

The secret of a really successful event, as I think everyone will agree, lies in the planning. Sometimes a lesson *may* be a success without any plan having been actually thought out and committed to paper, if the teacher is sufficiently experienced and alive to the needs of her pupil, but it is likely to be much more of a success – even with such experience and awareness – if proper planning has taken place. Sometimes the plans have to be abandoned if something untoward crops up, but this is immaterial compared with the loss of the pupil's interest and motivation that can occur if the lesson sags.

Another point should perhaps be taken into consideration: a teacher taking on any pupil is making a fairly long-term commitment. In order to maintain her own interest in a dyslexic pupil, who may well have several difficulties that will hinder his making rapid progress, it is essential that she makes plans and keeps detailed notes. The more one plans, and the more thought one gives to one's pupil, the more fascinating teaching him becomes. One thing leads to another, ideas begin to fly and the pupil's progress is seen in an entirely different light.

This chapter includes some guidelines for planning and evaluating lessons.

The piano is, of course, only one of the many musical instruments that a dyslexic may choose to learn. There are others that, for some dyslexics, would be more suitable, and are perhaps more congenial anyway. The relative values of other instruments for a dyslexic are discussed, and there are a few comments on the dangers and also the advantages of performance on any of them.

Finally, there are some thoughts on the place of music in the field of dyslexia and some speculation about the future for dyslexic musicians.

Useful equipment

There is a certain amount of equipment that it is handy to have at the ready for lessons with dyslexics. It has all been mentioned already in earlier chapters but here is a complete list:

Tape-recorder   (Chapter 3)
Plastic or wooden letters   "
Large photocopies of the music to be studied   (Chapter 4)
White ink eradicator   "
White self-stick labels   "
Coloured highlighters   "
Coloured 'post-it' labels   "
Adjustable frame   "
Coloured acetate sheets   "
Clear plastic sleeves   "
Washable overhead projector pen   "
Jumbo-sized manuscript paper   "
Life-size keyboard picture (A4 size)   (Chapter 5)
Rhythmic symbol flashcards   "
Felt-tip pens   "
Coloured adhesive paper dots   "
Tiddlywinks   "
(Velcro stickers)   "
Photocopies of sight-reading exercises   (Chapter 6)
Scissors   "
Glue   "
Cardboard backing for photocopies   "
Pencil grip   (Chapter 7)
Pens, pencils (B or HB), erasers   "
Good quality (coloured) manuscript paper   "
Plasticine   "
Rice tray   "
Rough paper   "
Cards with note and rest symbols   "
Indexed notebook for Italian terms   "
Star stickers   "

Planning a lesson

The music teacher is in a remarkably privileged position with regard to her pupils. Any constraints such as examinations or performances are, for the most part, self-imposed or pupil-instigated, and the overriding aim of a course of music lessons must surely be the enjoyment of music. Can this be achieved, though, without the pupil feeling that he is progressing? The dyslexic is, by definition, not a slow learner, and unless he feels that he is gradually improving, will he not suffer the same frustrations over his music as he may over other more 'academic' subjects?

I have heard it said that a dyslexic is usually not ambitious for prowess in music lessons; he is happy to jog along getting nowhere as long as he is not pressurized; the music lesson is an escape for him into a completely different world. Occasionally, that may be so, but I believe that it is much more common to come across the dyslexic who, whilst not comparing his own progress with that of his peers, is nevertheless keen to prove to himself and perhaps to his family that he can succeed in the field of music.

With this general aim – enjoyment and success – in mind for the dyslexic pupil, one has to construct a very gently sloping ladder of objectives, always remembering that what was taught the previous week will have to be revised and practised again, possibly many times, before it can be used as a platform for teaching something new. It may have to be completely retaught if it has been forgotten during the week – one has to be prepared for that – and one has to be ready to teach the same point in a different way.

Trying to fit everything that ought to be done into every lesson is almost always a bit of a nightmare. How the music teacher envies those teachers of other subjects who see their charges several times a week! We generally give our pupils one lesson a week, during which time we can sometimes do little more than hear what they have practised since their last lesson and give them pointers on how to overcome particular difficulties in the work for the week to come.

If it is possible, it is preferable by far to give a dyslexic two short lessons rather than one long one. A week may be too long a time for him to be expected to remember the salient points he has been taught. He usually does not have the opportunity to practise in the classroom the skills that he has learnt in the music lesson. If the environment in which he spent most of his time gave him the opportunity to apply and reinforce what he learned in the music lesson, perhaps one long lesson a week would be more acceptable. As it is, the more frequently we can see a dyslexic for a short lesson, the better.

If the teacher sees her pupil only once a week, she is very conscious of the fact that, if she forgets an important point or does not find time to do it, her pupil will have to manage on his own for two weeks instead of the usual one. She therefore tries hard to encompass everything in the one lesson. There is a lot for the pupil to remember. Two shorter lessons offer the opportunity to reinforce more frequently anything that is likely to be forgotten, while at the same time allowing for a more relaxed attitude on the part of the teacher. She knows that if she misses out something such as aural training she will have another opportunity to include it within a few days, instead of having to wait a whole week. So both the teacher and the pupil benefit.

In the limited time that is available, which can vary from as little as half an hour, or even less, to as much as an hour, a music teacher has, for all pupils, to fit in work on:

1.   technique: usually scales and arpeggios, as well as technical studies;
2.   sight-reading;
3.   aural training;
4.   repertoire;
5.   theory.

The assiduous teacher who conscientiously tries to fit all this in may be doing extremely well, but she may be neglecting the very thing which a *dyslexic* needs most of all: the warmth of open understanding of him as a *person* in an unhurried atmosphere.

When planning a lesson, one has to be prepared for everything one has planned to be abandoned in favour of what may amount to 20 minutes of listening and quiet counselling followed by a few favourite duets. If this happens, it should not be seen as a wasted lesson, and one should not feel guilty about having accepted money for a lesson that apparently had no progress to show for it. It is a valuable contribution to the welfare of any dyslexic that he should feel that he has allies in the world who are prepared to accept him as he is and help him to work out how to cope with life. So things may go 'wrong', but allowing for this eventuality should not prevent careful preparation for an ideal lesson.

Every lesson should build on what has gone before, it should be as multisensory as possible, it should be aimed at utilizing his strengths and it should address his weaknesses.

Planning a lesson in this way is only possible if one has made a very careful assessment of what those strengths and weaknesses are. As soon as possible after taking on a dyslexic as a pupil, or, alternatively, discovering that one's pupil has dyslexic tendencies, it is advisable to start making a list of his strengths and weaknesses. Constant reference can be made to the list in order to plan the most useful lesson, avoiding too much emphasis on his weaknesses and, whatever else happens, using his strengths to end the lesson on an upbeat note.

Assessments made by other people can certainly be helpful, but there is no substitute for careful observation made by oneself. Sometimes what someone else has noted in a classroom situation – perhaps difficulty with tracking – does not appear to cause a problem at all when tracking across a page of music is at stake. One can only speculate on the reason for this, no real research having been done on the subject, but it is certainly worth verifying findings by others before making any assumptions.

Because of the short attention span which so many dyslexics have, it is advisable to be ready with too much to do in the lesson rather than too little. It does not matter if all that has been planned is not done, but one does need to be one step ahead, even if the lesson is essentially pupil-led, in that his needs, his difficulties, his way of thinking about his instrument and his perception of the music are all paramount.

Focusing his concentration is hard for a dyslexic. He needs short bursts of attention to one particular point followed by a résumé – preferably by him – and then a break. If his attention snaps and he appears not to be listening, or not to understand, it can sometimes be because he has tired of the sound of his teacher's voice. Anyone who has undergone speech training for the stage will tell you how important it is to vary the pitch, speed and intensity of the voice if the audience's attention is to be held throughout a long speech. The piano pupil has to endure his teacher's voice alone for a whole lesson, so it can give him relief if she makes it as interesting as possible – within limits. The constantly varying voice can be as distracting as the flat monotone is boring.

If there is a particular difficulty, it is helpful to prepare beforehand by breaking the problem down into really minute steps, rather than hope for the best and start breaking it down if it does not seem to be going right. For example, if a scale has to be learnt with both hands together an octave apart, there will come a moment when one hand has to tuck the thumb under while the other hand simply plays the adjacent finger. Even if the pupil knows the fingering for each individual hand well, it may be sufficient for the first week of trying it with hands together just to go as far as the tuck under and no further. The scale can also be practised in contrary motion as far as the tuck-under – this time with both hands – or down from the top with the tuck-under in the left hand alone. The following week, one can then plan for the next step, but only if he can remember how to do the first step; careful revision will be needed first.

If the dyslexic has a poor visual memory but a good auditory memory, it will be helpful for him if what he has to remember for next week has been sung as well as seen on the page or felt as a tactile experience. When planning the lesson, one needs to leave enough time to reinforce the learning of each little bit with as much aural stimulation as possible. Hearing alone is not enough: singing comes from within and is more positive. If he has heard himself sing 'Lah–lah–lah–tuck', or whatever words are being used, he is more likely to remember it.

Alternatively, if his visual memory is one of his strengths, it is worth leaving enough time for *him* to write the notes of the passage to be practised with the appropriate fingering. This could be another use of the jumbo-sized manuscript paper in a plastic sleeve and an overhead projector pen. Be ready with an enlarged photocopy as well: the fingering can be discussed and he can write it in.

Life-sized pictures of the keyboard are invaluable. Slipped into a plastic sleeve they can be used again and again, combined with coloured paper stickers on which can be written fingering numbers (see Chapter 5). All this takes time, which is so precious, but it is *not* a *waste* of time. If it means that the pupil goes away happy and sure that he knows what and how to practise for next time, it will have been a good, useful lesson.

Evaluating the lesson

When the lesson is over, it is vital to have a few minutes to write down a quick evaluation of how it went. If it is possible, it is a good idea to arrange a dyslexic's lesson to come just before a natural break in the timetable, instead of having another pupil hard on his heels.

There will be much to note down later which will be of value when it comes to planning the next lesson. What was his general attitude like? Was he keen to show you what he had done, or was he diffident and slow to begin? What from the previous lesson had caught his imagination? What had he forgotten? You will need to think about why it had been forgotten and work out a more memorable way of teaching it, or plan the next lesson better so that that point has a more prominent place.

Dyslexics tend to have difficulty sometimes in changing from one task to another. It is useful to record the order in which the lesson has been conducted and to note how easily the pupil has been able to adjust to new tasks. Here is another good reason for organizing two short lessons instead of one long one. The natural break after the first lesson ensures that the pupil arrives at his next lesson with a fresher mind.

He may also be having this problem – difficulty in changing tasks – in his practising times, in which case it can be helpful to give him a planned timetable for practice each day, varying the order from day to day so that he does not always start with his favourite activity and then find himself unable to switch to other things that need practising. It is not enough to tell him to do this himself, he needs real help to organize himself.

There appears to be no generally accepted reason for suggesting that several short practices are more beneficial than one long practice. It is, however, noticeable to any music teacher that the pupil who practises regularly for 20 minutes a day progresses much better than the pupil who thinks he has done his practice if he has sat at his instrument for the whole of Sunday afternoon! Lessons therefore need to contain within them some specific help with practising for the week ahead, and records should be kept as to how he is coping with his practising.

Every indication of stress during the lesson should be recorded, and the reason for it should have careful consideration. Sometimes it may be very minor – frustration perhaps at having forgotten to bring some of his music. It is always worth having photocopies of all his music handy for such an eventuality. Sometimes it may be something at home, or even bullying at school, that is causing stress. He may need to talk about it, and, in the case of bullying his parents should be informed.

Every evaluation should include an appraisal of what went well and why. Conclusions reached can then be utilized and similar methods expanded next time, so that one gradually learns which methods of teaching are most suitable for that particular pupil.

Relative values of other instruments beside the piano

This is a field in which I can only pass on information I have gleaned from colleagues and fellow teachers. In talking to them, I have been struck by the similarity of the difficulties that their dyslexic pupils have to the difficulties of dyslexic piano pupils. This encourages one to believe that methods of alleviation of those difficulties are likely to be the same. Many relate to the score and these are typical of problems that have already been discussed (Chapter 3).

String players quite often have an additional problem with certain fingering patterns. When faced with a chromatic scale in a conventional scale book, a dyslexic tends to decide immediately that it is quite unfathomable, but if the following fingering is discussed and taught first, then everything falls into place on three strings out of four:

	1st string	2nd string
Going up	01 — 12 — 234	01 — 12 — 23
Going down	32 — 21 — 10	432 — 21 — 10

The line shows where the fingers slide one semitone.

The same teacher of the violin, who showed how a chromatic scale can be simplified, also suggested that dyslexic pupils who have difficulty with fingering for scales respond better when finger patterns are drawn for them (Figure 8.1).

The solid circle refers to a whole bow, the empty circles to a half bow, which means that the rhythm is also depicted. When the pupil has mastered this pattern with its accompanying rhythm, the teacher uses colour to show the notes that are sharps, drawing the same pattern three times but starting first on the G string, then on the D string and finally on the A string. Now the pupil knows (1) the rhythm, (2) where the tones and semitones are, (3) which notes are sharps, and therefore (4) why the key signatures are as they are. It is only at this point that she introduces the written music.

The pattern shown in Figure 8.2 can be used for the first three harmonic minor scales (D, G and A).

These useful finger patterns all help to limit eye activity, throwing the emphasis of the scale pattern onto the sound of the tones and semitones. Arpeggios can be learnt in the same way, either by learning the fingering sequence:

G major	020	313	2	313	020
G minor	0♭20	3♭13	2	3♭13	0♭20

or by using finger pattern pictures again. Both methods approach the learning of the arpeggio by *doing* it first and *hearing* the result before any attempt is made at

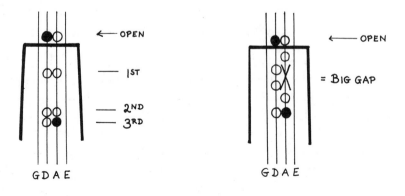

Figure 8.1   **Figure 8.2**

understanding the notation. The pupil's confidence in himself receives a substantial boost. It is interesting to note that there are fewer literacy problems in Japan if children are taught *kanjis*, which are pictorial representations, than if they are taught the *kana*, which are phonetic symbols representing syllables (Miles and Miles, 1990).

If a dyslexic pupil is not progressing very well on the first instrument of his choice, it may be sensible to move to another instrument, in which case it might be a good idea to consider how many notes are usually written for the new instrument in orchestral or band works. The violinist has the most notes to play of all the stringed instruments, whereas the double bass player usually has the fewest. Dyslexics with impaired spatial aptitude may have difficulty on the 'cello and double bass with the concept that the *lower* the left hand is on the string the *higher* the sound will be, so choosing a stringed instrument that is usually given fewer notes to play than a violin may not necessarily be the answer.

Wind instruments offer a good alternative to the piano or strings, and, in general, the same principle applies of numbers of notes being relative to the pitch of the instrument. The clarinet may prove difficult because of overblowing at the twelfth, and beware the bassoon! It has such a large range and so many different fingerings that what it gains in simplicity and number of notes that the player is likely to be asked to play, it loses in other complications.

Instruments that only need knowledge of one clef are, for the most part, the easiest. The recorder and the saxophone have much to recommend them, particularly as they both overblow at the octave, but, for those who may enjoy group music-making, brass instruments have the advantage of relying more than other instruments on the lips rather than on fingering. Finger action is reduced to the minimum, connections being made from the ear to the lips rather than from the ear to the fingers.

All wind instruments have a fixed hand position, although fingering may vary considerably. This fixed position seems to engender a feeling of stability that pianists and, to a certain degree, string players do not have. It would seem therefore that dyslexics with poor spatial aptitude might do better on a wind instrument, provided that the very important point of transposing instruments is taken into consideration. Problems can arise with any instrument that transposes, such as the clarinet, which has already been mentioned, the trumpet in B♭, the horn in F, and so on.

The harp is a very individual instrument and the music for it often looks very black and very fluid. Harpists tend to read by the shape of what they see; consequently dyslexics with problems over seeing patterns might not find the music easy to read, whereas the grid system used for a guitar and similar stringed instruments is relatively simple.

Percussion instruments are very difficult, as is the organ, because of the many things that have to be coordinated and the complexities of the score. However, it is not unknown for percussion players in the field of popular music to be dyslexic, and a dyslexic organ pupil recently succeeded in learning the whole of a

Mendelssohn organ sonata. It would seem that if a pupil has a feeling for a particular instrument, nothing else will do instead, and in the end his determination
and dedication will see him through.

Perhaps the easiest instrument of all for a dyslexic to study is the human voice,
singing being the most natural form of music-making. There is one main draw-
back: singing inevitably means familiarity with language and singers are often
required to sing not only in their native tongue, but also in foreign languages. This
means that every word has to be taught and learnt phonetically. As every vowel
and consonant of the English language comes under scruitiny anyway when
learning singing, this does not necessarily cause a problem, but it is something that
should be borne in mind at the outset.

Examinations and performances

The whole area of examinations for dyslexics is one which is presently undergoing
sympathetic review. There are now special provisions for dyslexic candidates exercised by all recognized examining boards. These are enormously helpful. Application should be made to the chosen examining board at the time of entry to find
out what is necessary in the way of an accompanying letter or certificate from an
educational psychologist or appropriately qualified specialist teacher. Because a
chosen examining board may amend its entry form requirements, current regula-
tions always need checking before making an application for a dyslexic candidate.

It is well worthwhile enquiring what provisions will be made for a particular
candidate, because these can sometimes vary according to the severity of the
dyslexia. The provisions can vary from a rearrangement of the normal order of
the examination to help with the choice of left or right hand for scales or arpeggios. Extra time can be allowed, especially for the preparation of sight-reading
and theory. In the case of theory examinations, the questions can be read to the
candidate by an amanuensis. Large print copies of sight-reading tests can be
provided, or the tests can be printed on coloured paper.

There are several schools of thought about the efficacy of taking examinations
and performing in public, whether the budding musician is dyslexic or not. If he is
dyslexic, other considerations have to be taken into account besides those which
normally apply, such as, is he capable of reaching the standard required to pass
comfortably, even on a bad day, and what will it do to his self-esteem if he fails?

There is a high-risk element in taking any practical examination. The dyslexic
performs best at all tasks when he is unstressed, and, on the day, much may depend
on the attitude of the examiner and the atmosphere in the examination room.

It is a great help if the pupil has had the opportunity to play on his instrument
beforehand in the room where the examination will take place. Acoustics can vary
so much, as can pianos, which will not only affect the pianist examinee but also
the sound of the accompaniment for a string or wind player. If it is not possible to
try out the sound and touch of the piano in the examination room, the next best
thing that can be done is to practise in as many other different locations as possi-

ble so that the pupil is prepared for things sounding and feeling different. This may also offer an insight into whether the examination is advisable or not. Will he take it in his stride?

Quite unexpected things can happen when a dyslexic's balance of mind is tested in an unfamiliar situation. John, taking the Grade 2 Associated Board piano examination, somehow succeeded in playing the sight-reading test right through with the clefs reversed so that what should have been played by the right hand was played by the left and vice versa. One cannot anticipate this sort of idiosyncratic behaviour; all one can do is to make quite sure that as high a standard as possible is reached in all prepared work so that if something goes completely topsy-turvy, there will be enough that goes right to counterbalance it.

Some practical examinations include a viva voce section. This, like sight-reading, can present the candidate with a truly testing situation, but as long as proper preparation has been done and the examiner is aware that the candidate is dyslexic, it should not be insuperably difficult.

Although the repercussions of failure should be carefully considered, the huge boost in confidence that follows on a successful pass is enormously valuable and often worth the risk. In fact, it can sometimes be the turning point in a dyslexic's development. It may be the first time that he has ever passed a public examination, and if this is so, it will certainly be the first time that he has been given a certificate to prove it. That certificate will mean a great deal to him.

Beginners may be much encouraged by the certificates that are issued to pupils who take the ABRSM preliminary grade examination. There is no pass/fail criterion and every examinee is given a certificate. It does not have the same kudos as a certificate that has to be earned by reaching a recognized standard, but it is nevertheless a form of recognition of a pupil's worth.

This recognition can also be earned by performance at a concert or competitive music festival. Many teachers like to encourage their pupils and give them something to work for by holding private, or even public, concerts. This is an opportunity for the pupil to earn a clap from the audience. The dyslexic is not used to being clapped – he is not the one who receives the prizes and acclamations on speech days – so every opportunity for performance where he can have his worth recognized will be a valuable boost to his self-esteem.

The performance does not have to be a solo – it can be a duet or even a trio – but great care has to be exercised to make sure that the dyslexic is not put in a position where the success of others depends upon his performance, as it would in a music festival. A duet with his teacher at a private concert is a gentle introduction to public performance. If something goes wrong, the teacher can cover up for him in a way that another pupil would probably not be able to do.

Dyslexic musicians and the future

Recognition of the effect that various characteristics of dyslexia may have on musicians is still in its infancy in comparison with recognition of the specific learning difficulties encountered in the classroom. We have compartmentalized the human being, with the result that there must be many people alive today who still have unanswered questions in their minds as to their apparent inability to succeed in playing a musical instrument sufficiently well, in spite of good intelligence and strongly musical leanings.

One such person known to me is a highly successful businessman, now retired, who builds superb harpsichords and keyboard instruments of all kinds, which are in great demand on the open market. It has puzzled him all his life that, in spite of enviable keyboard dexterity, he has been unable to master any relatively simple contrapuntal music. Nor is he capable of transposing onto the keyboard any of the well-known tunes that are constantly in his head. He can instantly detect a mistake in the tune or the harmony, and yet, in spite of his long association with the keyboard, he simply cannot work these tunes out for himself. Had he known, when he was younger, that his atrocious spelling was due to dyslexia and that dyslexia has many other manifestations, some of which would affect his ability to play contrapuntal music on the piano, he claims that his whole approach would have been different.

It would be nice to think that, had the right teaching been available to him, he might now be able to play a Bach fugue. Perhaps that is too fanciful, but recognition of the cause of his difficulties would not only have saved him much frustration, but would also have set him thinking about more positive ways of solving his problems. Instead of facing a brick wall of incomprehension, the whole enterprise might have become more like a game of fox and goose: he and his difficulties pitted against one another. Such an ingenious thinker would surely have outwitted his opponent many times.

As knowledge of dyslexia and its associated problems becomes more widely known, teachers of all subjects begin to apply their knowledge to their own field. Colleges and academies of music now recognize that a student may have much to offer despite his dyslexia and that he should be given as much help as possible. This attitude is reflected not only in the provisions for both internal and external examinations, but also in the pastoral care that dyslexic students receive.

Unwillingness to recognize dyslexia is not always the fault of the teacher. We have already seen how parents in particular can be resistant to the idea. By the time a pupil leaves school to go to music college, he too may easily persuade himself into thinking that, because he has achieved his ambition to be accepted to study music, he can now manage on his own without specific help. He is often anxious to put his dyslexia behind him as if it were a disease with a stigma attached to it, which has now been cured.

The assistant registrar for admissions to the Royal College of Music in London tells me that the biggest problem he has with dyslexics is in getting them to declare their dyslexia. He and the authorities in his college are ready to 'fall over themselves to help', if only they are given the proper information.

The truth is that dyslexic musicians, artists and craftsmen are often outstandingly good at their art. They seem to have an affinity with it which the non-dyslexic person will never achieve, however hard he may try. When a teacher is lucky enough to have a dyslexic of this calibre to teach, she can only be extremely grateful.

Throughout this book, we have been discussing almost exclusively how a music teacher can help a dyslexic to learn about *music*. We have looked at how dyslexia may affect the learning of a musical instrument, and there have been a few suggestions for getting round the obstacles that dyslexia seems sometimes to present. The aim has been to encourage the music teacher, and thereby the pupil, with the ultimate aim of fruitful music lessons and a happy relationship between them.

Every now and again, there has been the suggestion that something of what goes on in the music lesson may rub off in the classroom. We have some scientific evidence that there is a correlation between aspects of musical *ability* and reading *ability* (Barwick et al., 1989), and Barwick also suggests that the possibility remains that musical training may aid the development of reading skills, but evidence is insufficient to suggest that some of the language difficulties that beset dyslexics might be circumvented were the dyslexic to undertake a series of instrumental music lessons. However, there is growing circumstantial evidence that exposure to music and practical music-making can have positive and encouraging results. One view is that the instrumental musician may, if he is sufficiently dedicated, practise playing his chosen instrument almost every day of the year without feeling that he is doing anything other than contributing to his own enjoyment. He practises his listening, looking and touching skills, all of which may be needed to combat his dyslexic tendencies. They may not help him to spell any better, but they may be involved in helping him to follow text and to write.

Another view is that the addition of a tonal element to learning to read and spell is of considerable benefit. Many teachers of kindergarten-age children are now implementing this idea, in some cases with marked success.

A third view is that music heals. It is not offered as a cure for dyslexia, but it is offered as a cure for the disturbance of spirit that dyslexia often brings. This cure is worth pursuing for its own sake, particularly because the springboard for a successful battle against a difficulty must surely be an untroubled mind. Music has something quite unique to offer the person who is disorientated, muddled and sometimes deeply upset. It also offers opportunity for success and giving pleasure to others that cuts across all boundaries of race, creed and class, and success, as we all know, not only breeds success but is also vital in building self-esteem.

Summary

If it is to be as successful as possible, every instrumental music lesson for a dyslexic must be carefully planned. Once the structure is there, with each small objective worked out so that the pupil is not overloaded, there should be room for plenty of flexibility and adjustment to the way in which that particular pupil learns best, always bearing in mind that he is not just 'a pupil' but a complicated personality who, more than most, needs time and space to develop. His strengths and weaknesses have to be constantly borne in mind. Evaluation of each lesson is the vital link that makes planning the next step possible.

Non-keyboard instrumentalists often have the same difficulties with the score that pianists have. They may also have particular difficulties related to their instrument, but, on the whole, instruments that only use one clef and one line of music are simpler than the piano.

Whatever instrument is chosen, it is likely that the question of performing may eventually arise. Both examinations and concerts have their advantages and disadvantages, which should be carefully considered before attempting any sort of performance. Dyslexia and how it may affect an examinee is now looked upon with much more understanding than it was even as little as 10 years ago, so it is strongly advised that, should a pupil wish to take an examination, full use should be made of the provisions for dyslexics.

The relationship between music and dyslexia is one which is only beginning to be explored. This exploration offers exciting possibilities, and it is greatly to be hoped that enough musicians and teachers, both dyslexic and non-dyslexic, will have enough time and energy to contribute to it. I am convinced that there is a great deal to be gained for us all.

There is still a long way to go, and there are many barriers to be broken down, not least among dyslexics themselves, but there is no doubt that, in the present climate of greater public interest in dyslexia and more sympathetic provision for dyslexics, the musician who has the will to succeed is likely to meet with every encouragement. Let us hope that in the music room he will have a haven where he can blossom and flourish.

Appendix: Repertoire

Because the repertoire requirements may differ widely from pupil to pupil, I will not attempt to produce a comprehensive list of useful learning material for dyslexics. There is really no adequate alternative to examining the music oneself with each individual in mind. This may be difficult for some teachers if they live far from a good music shop and have to rely on mail order, so it is with those teachers in mind that I have compiled the following list. I have used much of the music myself but not all of it. In choosing the books that I have not had the opportunity to use, I have borne four things in mind:

1. clarity of presentation;
2. size of print;
3. amount of reading matter (other than music);
4. simplicity of musical construction.

I have not been beguiled by a multiplicity of colourful illustrations, because ultimately I have not found that these do anything more than distract. A *few* can enhance the product, and, in rare cases, such as the delightful pin men in Edna Mae Burnam's *A Dozen a Day* series, they can be positively helpful towards better performance, but on the whole it is the presentation of the music itself that is going to be the crucial factor.

I have not yet found a piano tutor book that can stand alone as a tutor for a dyslexic. Some of the many excellent tutors on the market have something to offer to a dyslexic, but they inevitably break down somewhere, and the financial outlay then seems excessive for the value that is received. They are also usually aimed at the younger child. The dyslexic pupil may need extremely simple material, but he is not going to react very well to being treated like a 5-year-old. If possible, the material used is best composed by the teacher who understands the likes and dislikes and also the difficulties that each pupil has.

Some of the most useful music on the market is in duet form, and I am sure that there will be much of this which other teachers know and I do not. Unfortunately one cannot guarantee that everything will stay in print, but some books of duets, for example. *Teacher and Pupil* (Löw) and *Lehrer und Schüler* (Ruthardt) have obviously stood the test of time so well that, even if they do go temporarily out of print, it is likely that they will reappear before very long.

Many well-known books of music contain one or two useful pieces for the dyslexic's repertoire. The following list is confined to those books of which at least half of the material might be suitable. As the pupil advances, so the teacher herself is going to be the best judge of suitable music for him, so I have not recommended any books beyond Grade 3 standard. On the whole, where choices have to be made, beware of contrapuntal music or music that leaps about too much, particularly in both hands at once. There are, however, some pieces by Bach, for instance, that are most useful: for example Preludes Nos 1 and 2 from the 'Twelve Little Preludes' or Prelude No 1 from the '48 Preludes and Fugues'.

Solo technique: Grade 0–5

A Dozen a Day, by Edna-Mae Burnam, published by International Music Publications Ltd, Southend Road, Woodford Green, Essex 1G8 8HN

Short technical exercises of gently graded difficulty. Very popular. Mini book from earliest beginning. Hands separately except for simple contrary motion work. Books 1–5 from simple five-finger exercise, hands together, to advanced technical agility. All exercises short enough to be memorized. Helpful illustrations. No reading material.

Practice Makes Perfect, by Pauline Hall and Paul Harris, published by Oxford University Press, Walton Street, Oxford OX2 6DP.

Musical technical exercises from Grade 1 to Grade 4 all in one book. Rather steeply graded, but transposition is advised and can be usefully practised on several exercises where it is not necessarily recommended. No illustrations but clearly presented. Some reading material.

Grade 0–1 solo repertoire

Tunes for Ten Fingers, and *More Tunes for Ten Fingers*, by Pauline Hall published by Oxford University Press, Walton Street, Oxford OX2 6DP.

These two books are aimed at the younger child. Progress is therefore slower than in the *Piano Time* series. The emphasis in the text is on learning the letter names of the notes, but this can be omitted if the pupil is adversely disposed towards letters. Illustrated in colour.

Piano Time 1 and *Piano Time Pieces 1*, by Pauline Hall published by Oxford University Press, Walton Street, Oxford OX2 6DP.

Piano Time 1 is a tutor starting conventionally from middle C with keyboard pictures to help. New notes are incorporated very quickly, two at a time, combined with semibreves, minims and crotchets, which, all together, can be confusing for a dyslexic, but there is some useful material for selective use. Minimal illustrations.

Piano Time Pieces 1 is intended as a supplement to *Piano Time 1*. All the pieces are for both hands but not necessarily for hands together at the same time. Minimal illustrations.

Blues and Boogies – The Best of Composition Challenge, edited by Maggie Teggin, Boosey Big Note Series No 12, published by Boosey & Hawkes Music Publishers Ltd, 295 Regent Street, London W1R 8JH.

Seventeen useful pieces clearly set out in large print. Many of these pieces adapt well to being taught from memory. Useful for the slightly older pupil who cannot manage hands together very well. No illustrations. Long book.

Scenes at a Farm, by Walter Carroll, published by Forsyth, 126 Deansgate, Manchester M3 2GR.

These old favourites still have appeal, but careful selection is advised. Particularly helpful for the recognition of intervals, both melodic and chordal; four simple duets at the end for equal partners but with the first player playing in octaves. No illustrations.

Easy Piano Entertainment, arranged by Hans-Günter Heumann, published by Bosworth & Co, 14/18 Heddon Street, Regent Street, London W1R 8DP.

Thirty pieces of popular repertoire in easy and very easy arrangements. There really is something for everyone here, from a simple arrangement of J.S. Bach's 'Musette' from the 'Notebook for Anna Magdalena Bach' to traditional folk songs, well-known orchestral music and tunes such as the 'Harry Lime Theme'.

The Technic Companion, by Denes Agay and Nancy Bachus published by Yorktown Music Press, distributed by Music Sales Ltd, 8/9 Frith St, London W1V 5TZ and Music Sales Corporation, 225 Park Avenue South, New York, NY 1003, USA.

This might be a useful book to use in conjunction with another. It emphasizes the pattern of black notes, and there is a teacher's accompanying part for almost everything. There is a lot of technique practice.

Grades 1–2

Five by Ten, Grade 1, edited and graded by Alec Rowley, published by Alfred Lengnick and Co Ltd, C/o William Elkin Music Services, Station Road Industrial Estate, Salhouse, Norwich NR13 6NY.

Thirty pieces by twentieth-century composers. The advantage that many of these pieces has is that the hand positions do not change throughout the piece. No illustrations.

Very First Classics, by edited by Donald Gray, published by Boosey & Hawkes Ltd, 295 Regent Street, London W1R 8JH.

Several useful pieces in this book, some of which are quite short. No illustrations.

That's A Good Tune. Fun Pieces for Piano by 12 Living Composers, published by Kevin Mayhew Ltd, Rattlesden, Bury St Edmunds, Suffolk IP30 0SZ.

Book 1 (out of 3) contains 15 witty and delightful pieces, several of which have an ostinati bass. A few would be too difficult for this grade. Colour illustrations by the cartoonist Roy Mitchell.

The Countryside, by Walter Carroll, published by Forsyth, 126 Deansgate, Manchester M3 2GR.

Not too much to think about in both hands at once here. More chordal work than in *Scenes at a Farm* and also more movement up and down the keyboard, but every move has some point of reference to link it to what has just been played. One duet. No illustrations.

Play it Again, Chester, vol. 1: Boogies, Rags and Blues for Piano, by Carol Barratt published by Chester Music, 8/9 Frith Street, London W1V 5TZ, distributed by Music Sales Ltd, Newmarket Road, Bury St Edmunds, Suffolk IP33 3YB.

These short pieces are for the pupil with a good sense of rhythm and a feel for the keyboard. Simply constructed for easy memorizing. Not more than one sharp or flat. No illustrations.

Grade 3

Five Miniature Preludes and Fugues, by Alec Rowley, published by Chester Music, 8/9 Frith Street, London W1V 5TZ, distributed by Music Sales Ltd, Newmarket Road, Bury St Edmunds, Suffolk IP33 3YB.

An excellent introduction for the intelligent dyslexic to both playing and listening to contrapuntal music. Every piece has one or two accidentals but on the whole the notes are not difficult. Preludes would stand alone. Simple, ingenious and very useful. No illustrations.

Sight-reading

Play at Sight – A Graded Sight Reading Course for Pianists, by Christine Brown, published by EMI Music Publishing Ltd, Southend Road, Woodford Green, Essex IG8 8HN.

More than anything else, sight-reading needs to be written especially for dyslexics, but as examinations approach, it is useful to have examples written by other people. These books offer more examples than many other books. No illustrations.

Duets

Teacher and Pupil, Book 1, by Löw vol. 472 of Schirmer's Library of Music Classics, published by G Schirmer, C/o Music Sales, New Market Road, Bury St Edmunds, Suffolk IP33 3YB.

Throughout this invaluable collection of 40 tuneful duets, there is a gradual progression from semibreves in the five-finger position, hands in octaves, to semiquavers and a few chords in keys up to two sharps or two flats. Exceptionally well graded, with sensitive arrangements of well-known classical and folk tunes, as well as original pieces. Primo part in the treble.

Lehrer und Schüler, by Adolf Ruthardt, published by C.F. Peters, 10–12 Baches Street, London N1 6DN.

Another very carefully, but more steeply, graded collection of 40 duets, including primo player in the bass as well as in the treble. Some of the secondo parts in the treble may be a little too musically interesting for the primo player in the bass. Never more than one sharp or flat in the key signature. Hands mostly in octaves.

Sonatinas on 5 Notes, Op. 163, by Anton Diabelli, edited by Peters Leipzig, published by Peters Edition, 10/12 Baches Street, London N1 6DN.

Not for the beginner or for a dyslexic reading at sight but, as the title suggests, reassuring for the pupil who needs to stay in one place unless he is to be confused. Primo largely plays with hands in octaves.

Two at the Piano, by Josef Gruber, edited by Fanny Waterman and Marion Harewood, published by Faber Music Ltd, 3 Queen Square, London WC1N 3AU.

Fifty graded duets, many of them very short but with repeats. The vast majority are in C major. Key signatures are not used for the primo part, but there are a few accidentals. Primo part mostly in octaves.

10 Rhythmical Dances, by Gerard Hengeveld, published by Broekmans & Van Poppel, Amsterdam-Z, Van Baerlestraat 92, Netherlands.

Modern ballroom dances, such as the rhumba, tango, paso doble, etc., with attractive harmonies and a strong catchy beat. These are for the older pupil. One berceuse cradle song at the end is entirely composed on black notes. No flat key signatures apart from this one.

Glossary

accelerando	gradually getting faster
accidental	a sharp or flat not included in the key signature. A natural sign may also be used to cancel a sharp or flat in the key signature
alphabetic	the phase in the acquisition of reading skills when the reader uses his knowledge of the sounds of the letters of the alphabet
articulation	method of play, whether smoothly (legato) or detached (shortened or staccato)
beam	a straight line joining together notes with the value of less than a crotchet
binocular control	the ability to converge the focus of the eyes to a single point
cadence	the end of a phrase where there is a point of rest or relaxation in the music
cadenza	a flourish of indefinite form
chromatic	implying the production of all the semitones
clef	the sign determining the pitch of the notes to be played 𝄞, 𝄢, 𝄡
cogwheeling	the result of an inability to progress the focus of the eyes smoothly from target to target
contrapuntal	music written according to the rules of counterpoint
counterpoint	the horizontal aspect of music. The chief interest lies in the various strands that make up the texture, in particular the combination of these strands and their relationship to each other and to the whole
cross lateral	normally when hand and eye are oppositely lateralized, for example right-handed but left-eyed. The term can also be used with reference to the laterality of the ears or feet

142

crotchet	a quarter-note ♩, i.e. half the value of a minim or half-note ♪, which is in turn half the value of a semibreve or whole note 𝄂
diatonic (scale)	that scale in which the interval of a tone is used. Both halves of the diatonic major scale consist of four notes, the first three being separated by the interval of a whole tone and the fourth note by the interval of a semitone
directional confusion	the confusion that can arise when there is uncertainty about left and right
dominant	the fifth note above the tonic
duple time	two beats (pulses) in a bar, the first being the stronger
dynamics	loudness or softness
dyspraxia	the impairment or immaturity of the organisation of movement
feminine ending	the final chord being weaker than the penultimate chord
fermata	a pause ⌒
flat	the sign used to lower the note by one semitone ♭
harmonic (minor)	the arrangement of the notes of the minor scale that remains constant whether ascending or descending
iconic	of, or pertaining to, an icon or picture
interval	the distance in pitch between two notes
inversion	the rearrangement of a chord so that one of the notes previously in the middle or at the top becomes the lowest note
key signature	the configuration of sharps or flats at the beginning of a piece of music that shows which notes are to be raised or lowered throughout the piece
kinaesthetic	to do with action and the feel of action
largo	slow, stately
laterality	the dominance of one or other side of limbs or organs of the body
leading note	the 7th note of the scale
legato	smooth, indicating no break between sounds
leger (ledger) lines	short additional lines to provide for notes that lie above or below the limits of the stave

logographic	the phase in the acquisition of reading skills when the reader guesses the word by its shape
melodic (minor)	the arrangement of the notes of the minor scale that differs in its descending form from its ascending form
mf (mezzo forte)	half or moderately loud
mixed laterality	when there is no dominance of laterality, for example when neither hand, eye, ear or leg appears to be dominant over its counterpart
modulation	the passing from one key to another. Music is said to be in the key of, for example, C major when the overwhelming majority of notes that are employed belong to the scale of C major. If there is a temporary shift of tonality to the key of, say, G major, the music is said to have modulated
motor control	muscular control of the limbs
natural	the sign denoting that a sharp or flat should be cancelled ♮
neurone	a nerve cell
ornament	a decoration or embellishment of the note
orthographic	the phase in the acquisition of reading skills when the reader uses his knowledge of all the rules and conventions that he has learnt
ostinati	a melodic figure occurring unchanged and at the same pitch throughout a composition or a section of a composition (Italian =obstinate, persistent)
overblowing	a special way of playing on wind instruments so that the upper harmonics are produced instead of the fundamental notes
perfect (cadence)	the progression from the dominant chord to the tonic chord at the end of a phrase
phonemic	to do with the smallest sounds made by letters of the alphabet
phonological	to do with the sounds of words
phototherapy	a medical term to do with the treatment of infantile jaundice and other complaints
phrase (phrasing)	the musical parallel to the way in which words are grouped together in language
presto	fast
quadruple time	four beats (pulses) in a bar ♪
quaver	a note of half the value of a crotchet

rallentando	gradually getting slower
rest	a sign used for silence ⁊
ritenuto	held back
root position	that position of the notes of a triad or chord that indicates that the note upon which it is built is at the bottom, or root.
saccades	rapid and irregular bounds made by the eyes when trying to follow a moving target
sequence (sequencing)	the repetition of a definite group of notes in different positions of the scale
sharp	the sign used to raise the note by one semitone ♯
sight-reading	performing a piece of previously unseen music with no opportunity to practise it
slur	a curved line joining two or more notes, indicating that there should be no break in the sound and that the final note should be slightly shortened
solfege	the teaching of the rudiments of music, including ear training as an indispensable factor
spatial	relating to the perception of space
staccato	detached, short
stave/staff	the five lines on which music is written
system	the collection of staves necessary for the complete score. Staves are bracketted together to form a system
tie	a curved line joining notes of the same pitch, indicating that only the first note is to be sounded
tonality	the result of the process of relating a series of notes or chords to a focal point that is called the tonic of the key
tonic	the first degree, or key note, of the scale
tracking	following one line of text
triple time	three beats (pulses) in a bar, the first being the strongest

Useful addresses

Associated Board of the Royal Schools of Music, 14 Bedford Square, London WC1B 3JG. Tel: 0171–636 5400

British Dyslexia Association, .98 London Road, Reading, Berkshire RG1 5AU. Tel: (01734) 662677

Guildhall School of Music and Drama, Silk Street (Examinations), Barbican, London EC2Y 8DT. Tel: 0171–628 2571

The Klavar Foundation of Great Britain, Klavar House, 171 Yarborough Road, Lincoln LN1 3NQ. Tel: (01522) 523117

The Orton Dyslexia Society Inc, 724 York Road, Baltimore, Maryland 21204, USA. Tel: 301–296–0232

Trinity College of Music, 13–15 Mandeville Place, London W1M 6AQ. Tel: 0171–935 5773

Educational suppliers

LDA (Learning Development Aids),Duke Street, Wisbech, Cambridgeshire PE13 2AE. Tel: (01945) 463441

Philip and Tacey Ltd, North Way, Andover, Hampshire SP10 5BA. Tel: (01264) 332171

For music on its side

Bold Beginnings by Eloise Ristad, published by Dorian Press, Box 1985, Boulder, CO 80306 USA.

Bibliography

Adler-Grinberg, D. and Stark, L. (1978). Eye movements, scan paths and dyslexia. *American Journal of Optometry and Physiological Optics* **55**, 557–70

Atkinson, J., Watkins, K. and Fowler-Watts, S. (1991). *The Musical Ability of Children with Dyslexia and its Relationship to Visual Function*. Unpublished Psychology Part II dissertation, University of Cambridge, in conjunction with Kings' College Choir School, Cambridge.

Atterbury, B.W. (1985). Psychology of music. In *Musical Differences in Learning-disabled and Normal-achieving readers*. **13** Psychology of Music, pp 114–123.

Ayres, A. J. with assistance from J. Robbins (1979). *Sensory Integration and the Child*. Los Angeles, CA: Western Psychological Services.

Bachmann, M-L. (1991). *Dalcroze Today – An Education through and into Music*. Oxford: Clarendon Press.

Badcock, D and Lovegrove, W. (1981). The effects of contrast, stimulus duration and spatial frequency on visual persistence in normal and specifically disabled readers. In Bouma, H. Kolers, P A. and Wrolstad M, (eds) *Processing of Visible Language*, Proceedings of Conference at Institute of Perception Research, IPO, Eindhoven.

Baddeley, A. (1990). *Human Memory: Theory and Practice*. Brighton: Lawrence Erlbaum.

Bakker, D. (1990). *Neuropsychological Treatment of Dyslexia*. Oxford: Oxford University Press.

Barwick, J., Valentine, E., West, R. and Wilding, J. (1989). Relations between reading and musical abilities. *British Journal of Educational Psychology*, **59**, 253–257.

Beard, R.M.(1969). *An Outline of Piaget's Developmental Psychology*. London: Routledge and Kegan Paul.

Bentley. A. (1966). *Musical Ability in Children and its Measurement*. London: Harrap.

Berard, G. (1993). *Hearing Equals Behaviour*. Connecticut: Keats Publishing.

Borchgrevink, H.M. (1982). Prosody and Musical Rhythm are controlled by the Speech Hemisphere In: M. Clynes (ed.) *Music, Mind and Brain – The Neuropsychology of Music*. New York: Plenum Press.pp 151–159.

Buck. P. (1944). *Psychology for Musicians*. Oxford: Oxford University Press.

Choksy, L. (1981). *The Kodaly Context – Creating an Environment for Musical Learning*. New Jersey: Prentice-Hall.

Clay, M.M. (1994). *Reading Recovery: The Early Detection of Reading Difficulties*. London: Heinemann

Clynes, M. (1982). *From Music, Mind and Brain – The Neuropsychology of Music*. New York: Plenum Press.

Cooke, D. (1959). *The Language of Music*. Oxford: Oxford University Press.

Delacato, C.H. (1971). *A New Start for the Child with Reading Problems*. Springfield, IL: Charles C. Thomas.

Erikson, C.W. and Collins, J.F. (1968). Sensory traces versus the psychological movement in the temporal organisation of form. *Journal of Experimental Psychology*, **77**: 376–382.

Fawcett, A.J., Pickering, S. and Nicolson, R.I. (1993). Development of the DEST Test for the early screening for dyslexia In: S.F Wright and R. Groner (eds) *Facets of Dyslexia and its Remediation*. Amsterdam: Elsevier. pp 483–493.

Frith, U. (1985). Beneath the surface of developmental dyslexia. In J.C, Marshall., K.E. Patterson, and M. Coltheart, (eds) *Surface Dyslexia in Adults and Children*. Brighton: Lawrence Erlbaum. pp. 301–330

Froseth, J. (1984). *Listen, Move, Sing and Play*. Michigan: Music Learning Research Division of G.I.A Publications Inc., University of Michigan School of Music.

Galaburda, A.M., Menard, M.T. and Rosen, G.D. (1994). Evidence for aberrant auditory anatomy in developmental dyslexia. *Proceedings of the National Academy of Sciences of the USA*, **91**, 8010–8013 Medical Sciences.

Gardner, H. (1983). *Frames of Mind – The Theory of Multiple Intelligencies*. London: Harper Collins.

Gathercole, S. E. and Baddeley, A.D. (1993). *Working Memory and Language: Essays in Cognitive Psychology*. Brighton: Lawrence Erlbaum.

Goulandris, A. and Snowling, M. (1991). Visual memory deficits: a plausible cause of developmental dyslexia? *Cognitive Neuropsychology* **8**, 127–154.

Hampshire, S. (1990). *Every Letter Counts*. London: Bantam Press.

Hornsby, B. (1988). *Overcoming Dyslexia. A Straightforward Guide for Families and Teachers*. London: Macdonald. Optima.

Hubicki, M. (1990). Learning difficulties in music. In: G. Hales (ed.) *Meeting Points in Dyslexia*. Reading: British Dyslexia Association. pp. 314–316.

Hubicki, M. (1991). A multisensory approach to reading music. In: *Dyslexia: Integrating Theory and Practice*. London: Whurr. pp. 322–328.

Hubicki, M. and Miles, T.R. (1991). Musical notation and multisensory learning. *Child Language Teaching and Therapy* **7** London: Edward Arnold.

Hugdahl, K. (ed.) (1988). *Handbook of Dichotic Listening: Theory, Methods and Research*. Chichester: John Wiley & Sons.

Hulme. C. and Snowling, M. (eds) (1994). *Reading Development and Dyslexia*. London: Whurr.

Jaques-Dalcroze, E. (1930). *Eurythmics, Art and Education*. London: Chatto and Windus.

Jaques-Dalcroze, E (1965). *Le Rhythme, la Musique and l'Education*. Lausanne: Foetisch.

Joudry, P. (1989). *Sound Therapy for the Walkman*. Dalmeny, Saskatchewan, Canada: Steele and Steele.

Karma, K. (1982). Musical, spatial and verbal abilities. A special report. *Psychology of Music*. Special Issue, pp. 69–71.

Kodály, Z. (1974). *The Selected Writings of Zoltan Kodály*. London: Boosey and Hawkes.

Lefroy, R. (1990). *Improving Literacy through Motor Development*. Palmyra, Western Australia: Dunsborough Enterprises Publications.

Lévi-Strauss, C. (1964). *The Raw and the Cooked – Introduction to a Science of Mythology*, 1. (translated by J. and D. Weightman). London: Jonathan Cape.

Lundberg, I., Frost, J. and Petersen, O. (1988). Effects of an extensive programme for stimulating phonological awareness in pre-school children. *Reading Research Quarterly* **33**, 263–284.

Macfarlane Smith, I. (1964). *Spatial Ability: its Educational and Social Significance*. London: University of London Press.

Mackworth, J.F. (1972). Some models of the reading process: learners and skilled readers. *Reading Research Quarterly* **7**, 701–733.

Mainwaring, J. (1933). Kinaesthetic factors in the recall of musical experience. *British Journal of Psychology* **23** (3), 284–307.

Marin, O.S.M. (1982). Neurological aspects of music perception and performance. In: Deutsch, D. (ed.) *The Psychology of Music*, Ch. 15. New York: Academic Press.

Matthay, T. (1926). *On Memorising*. Oxford: Oxford University Press.

Mattingley, I.G. (1972). Reading, the linguistic process, and linguistic awareness. In: J.F.Kavanagh and I.G. Mattingley (eds) *Language by Ear and by Eye: the Relationship Between Speech and Reading* pp. 133–147. Cambridge, MA: MIT Press.

Miles, T. and Miles, E. (1983). *Help for Dyslexic Children*. London: Routledge.

Miles, T. and Miles, E. (1990). *Dyslexia: a Hundred Years on*. Oxford: Oxford University Press.

Mills, J.I. (1984). The pitch subtest of Bentley's measure of musical abilities. *Psychology of Music* **12** , 94–105.

Pavlidis, G.Th. and Miles, T.R. (eds) (1981). *Dyslexia Research and its Application to Education.* Chichester: John Wiley & Sons.

Penfield, W. (1954). Studies of the central cortex of man. A review and an interpretation. H.W. Magoun, (ed.). *Brain Mechanisms and Consciousness* In: Oxford: Blackwell. pp. 284–309.

Peters, R.S. (1958). *The Concept of Motivation.* London: Routledge.

Posner, M.I. and Konick, A.W. (1966). On the role of interference in short term retention. *Journal of Experimental Psychology* **72**, 221–231.

Pribram, K.H. (1982). Prolegomena for a theory of the meaning of meaning. In: M. Clynes (ed.) *Music, Mind and Brain – the Neuropsychology of Music,* New York: Plenum Press. pp. 21–36.

Ristad, E. (1982). *A Soprano on her Head: Right-side-up Reflections on Life and Other Performances.* Utah: Real People Press.

Samama, A. (1981). *Muscle Control for Musicians.* Utrecht: Bohn, Scheltema and Holkema.

Shuter-Dyson, R. and Gabriel, C. (1981). *The Psychology of Musical Ability,* 2nd edn. London: Methuen.

Sloboda, J. (1986). *The Musical Mind: The Cognitive Psychology of Music.* Oxford: Oxford Science Publications.

Snowling, M. and Thomson, M. (eds) (1992). *Dyslexia: Integrating Theory and Practice.* London: Whurr.

Stanley, G. and Hall, R. (1973). Short term visual information processing in dyslexics. *Child Development.* **44**, 841–844.

Stones, E. (1966). *An Introduction to Educational Psychology.* London: Methuen.

Storr, A. (1992). *Music and the Mind.* London: Harper–Collins.

Thomson, M.E. (1990). *Developmental Dyslexia: Its Nature, Assessment and Remediation,* 3rd edn. London: Whurr.

Tomatis, A.A. (1991). *The Conscious Ear.* New York: Station Hill Press.

Vellutino, F.R., Steger, J.A., Desetto, L. and Phillips, F. (1975). Immediate and delayed recognition of visual stimuli in poor and normal readers. *Journal of Experimental Child Psychology* **19**, 223–232.

Vernon, M.D. (1962). *The Psychology of Perception.* London: Pelican.

Vernon, P.E. (1961). *The Structure of Human Abilities,* 2nd edn. London: Methuen.

Warnock, M. (1987). *Memory.* London: Faber & Faber.

Wilkins, A.J. (1986). What is visual discomfort? *Trends in Neurosciences.* **August,** 343–6.

Wisbey, A. (1980). *Learning through Music.* Lancaster: M T Press.

Index